Film and Television Textual Analysis

A Teacher's Guide

Keith McDonald

Auteur

Keith McDonald

teaches English Literature and English Language at York College. He is a contributor to the online film journal, *Scope*, and is completing a PhD in AIDS and Representation.

Acknowledgements

Thanks to Vanessa Clare and John Sylph for their advice and support.

First Published 2005
by Auteur

The Old Surgery, 9 Pulford Road, Leighton Buzzard, Bedfordshire LU7 1AB. Tel: 01525 373896

© Auteur Publishing, 2005

ISBN 1 903663 53 9

Auteur on the internet: http://www.auteur.co.uk

Designed and typeset by Active Media Publishing, PO Box 737, Cottenham, Cambridge CB4 8BA

Printed by The Direct Printing Company, Saxon Fields, Old Harborough Road, Brixworth, Northants, NN6 9BX

Contents

Getting Started

1.1 Defining 'texts'

This chapter will cover some of the key concepts involved in close textual analysis of the moving image, which can be applied to any media text. The terms text and textual analysis are used in reference to overarching concepts. A text is any cultural or societal product or document, and the term can be applied to everything from Shakespeare's *Hamlet*, to a Jamie Oliver recipe, Orson Welles' **Citizen Kane** (1941) to the *Ten O'clock News*. In Film Studies, the term is often used to describe a film itself, the script, or any critical work surrounding the medium. In Media Studies, the term is used in a broader sense, and can be applied to everything from a printed advertisement for a hair care product to *EastEnders*. Texts are best understood as 'documents' that can be presented to an audience for a whole range of purposes over a number of genres. The practice of close textual analysis is also referred to as Structuralism or Formalism, which is a school of thought that is interested in analysing the technical aspects of how film works.

Three basic questions should be asked when considering texts. These are:

- What is the text?
- What meaning do we find in it?
- What tools have we used to find this meaning?

Textual analysis involves the study of a given text in order to 'read' the way in which it has been constructed for an audience. The process of textual analysis involves identifying the codes and conventions of a text and decoding or reading them. This includes recognising the language of a moving image, as in the ways in which it is put together on the screen, and the analysis of what that language is telling the audience. For example, if a film-maker wishes to create a film set in London during the Victorian era, they will need to do far more than simply dress their actors in Victorian era clothing and have them speak in cockney accents! In establishing the tone and setting of the film they will need to consider the sights and sounds of the period, the way in which the film is edited and the way in which characters are filmed in their environment. Crucially, the ability to decode the ways in which this is put together can tell us something about how film-makers perceive their subject matter, and how they think their audience perceives that subject matter. This relies upon the concept that in taking part in textual analysis, we can learn something about the culture that has produced it.

Textual analysis involves investigating how a text is working and why it is working in such a way. It is important to realise that there are multiple meanings that can be found in a text, and that these meanings are by no means fixed. Two individuals may take away entirely different meanings from a text, depending on their relationship with the material and (among other things) whether it is intended to mean something to them. Let's take a recent example of how a film can work in this way. Mel Gibson's **The Passion of The Christ** (2004) is a film that provokes strong emotional responses, but these responses are by no means guaranteed to be consistent from one audience member to another. Each will bring their own personal experiences and beliefs to the film and therefore a multitude of meanings can be derived from the text itself.

This Guide will be focusing on textual analysis of the moving image in order to fully explore the theory and practice of it. It will cover a range of texts and the ways in which each works in its own genre. Most of us are subjected to a range of images at an increasingly heightened pace. In the information age, we are bombarded with moving images all fighting for space in the cultural wilderness. The upsurge in moving images has been rapid, and we increasingly live in the age of the image itself. Consider the range of moving images we can expect to see in a typical morning:

When eating our breakfast we switch on the television to be entertained by celebrity interviews, or to catch up on the news and weather (or to be influenced by advertisers to buy their products). Before we have left our homes, the media has informed, entertained and attempted to persuade us. We have been an audience to three types of text before the day has begun. These programmes are strategically placed to fit our needs. For example, it makes sense to have news and weather at key points in the day. Notice the frequency of news bulletins on the BBC early in the morning. This is obviously intended to target a high number of people for only a short time as they hurry to leave their homes.

The television companies are acutely aware of audiences at this time. Consider for example, the importance of children as audiences when they are being entertained at key points in the day. The advertising around children's programmes specifically targets them as consumers who can use that all-important 'pester power' to buy McDonalds' Happy Meals, soft drinks, toys and merchandising.

Making Meaning

Textual analysis exists in order to highlight the strategies and techniques that the media uses to convey meaning to us, and to uncover the message behind the image. This is not as easy as it may sound. For example, textual analysis would be a simple job if it were used only to consider the production of individual texts made for individual audiences for sole purposes. This would be akin to trying to understand a moving image made using a mobile phone and transmitted from one friend to another. The media is obviously far more complex than this and is fractured into a multitude of genres, each with unfixed strategies that change over time. We must consider the text itself of course, and there are specific tools of analysis that allow us to decode moving images, as shall be demonstrated. However, there are other factors to consider that make matters more complicated. In looking at (reading) a given text, we can look beyond what is on the screen. We can also consider the contextual factors that govern the mode of production. In considering the mode of production that influences a text, the following questions can be asked:

- What individuals are involved in the text's production?
- What media institutions are involved in the text's production?
- When was it produced?
- Who was it produced for?
- Why was it produced?
- What does this tell us about the producer?

What we are all trying to do when we view an image is find meaning within it, and most often the producer of the image is attempting to provide meaning to an audience. As narrators, they seek to create an image to be decoded and understood; as narratees, we seek to read the image and decode what it is telling us. What follows are some ways in which meaning can be considered with regards to textual analysis.

It has been suggested that there are types of 'reading' that can be applied to a text. These are:

- **Dominant reading:** Here, the viewer fully shares the text's codes and accepts the intended reading. For example, a viewer of Oliver Stone's *JFK* (1991) may wholly endorse the film-maker's vision of events.
- **Negotiated reading:** In this case, the viewer partially accepts the codes of the texts, but may be critical of certain aspects. For example, a viewer may feel sympathetic to the characters in Steven Spielberg's *Saving Private Ryan* (1998); yet remain critical of perceived biases of the version of history presented.
- **Oppositional reading:** Here the viewer understands the intended meaning of a text, but rejects, and is critical of, it and its producers. For example, a viewer may view *JFK* as wrongly perpetuating conspiracy theories, or view *Saving Private Ryan* as a piece of revisionist history.

Another way to consider meaning can be:

- **Explicit meaning:** This meaning is at the foreground of an image or representation that we are intended to see without much difficulty. For example, a man walks down a busy street, a straightforward image.
- **Implicit meaning:** This is a subtler message that can be read in different ways. The man walking down the street is facing a crowd of people all walking in the opposite direction – does this indicate his struggle against the masses?
- **Subtext:** This meaning can be read into a text, and often stems from criticism. Subtexts are often a matter of debate and can be contentious. For example, some have argued that a film such as *The Lord of the Rings* (2001) has a problematic subtext, in that it presents a huge battle between races in which the dark skinned characters are presented as evil.

Meaning can also be derived from a text on the following two levels:

- **Denotative level:** This is the straightforward visual image that we see on the screen. Consider the way the Bates family home is famously shot in *Psycho* (1960). On a denotative level, we simply see a house on a hill at night.

- **Connotative level:** This is the meaning that we associate with the image that we see. On a connotative level, we perceive the house in *Psycho* ominously, filled with dread and horror.

A large amount of classic film theory is focused on semiotics, that is, the semantic system of images, words and sounds. This can be identified in the following terms:

- **Sign:** That is, an image in the raw. A carving knife, for example, is simply a metal implement.
- **Signifier:** In the context of a scene involving a murder in a shower, this knife signifies death and violence. However, in a scene filmed in a restaurant kitchen, it is no longer a symbol of such dread.

Meaning can change over time. Advance teaser trailers for Sam Raimi's *Spider-Man* (2002) contained images of the hero trapping a helicopter in his webbing between the twin towers of the World Trade Center. For obvious reasons, these images were removed after the attacks of 11 September 2001, because we now associate the twin towers with different connotations.

Advertisers are acutely aware of the connotations we associate with images and are keen to show their product in a positive light, or as having positive connotations. Think of an image of a brand new car cutting through traffic with ease. The connotations here are: traffic is bad and troublesome, this car is good and frees you up. What is interesting here is the 'you' who is being addressed. In the case of advertisements we should consider who the target is. What should be remembered is that advertisements do not appear on our screens at random, but are selected according to the audience that the advertiser has in mind. As advertisements are shown around programmes, they often seek to appeal to the imagined viewer of a given show. Take the advertising seen during and around a programme such as Channel 4's *Countdown*. You are likely to see a mix of advertisements for low cost loans, stair lifts and Pot Noodle: this is because the advertisers assume (and their research supports this) that the audience for *Countdown* is made up of retired people and students. Therefore, if you look at the advertising around *Sex and the City* and *Footballer's Wives* you will see adverts for hair care and beauty products, whereas powerful cars and razors will be sold around *The Sopranos* and *Star Trek*.

Let's take a classic example of how an audience can be targeted and consider this in a contemporary context.

Case Study – Oxo

Oxo television campaigns from ...

the 1960s ...   *and the 1980s*

(stills © The Advertising Archives)

This is recognised as an iconic campaign that is testament to the power of simple advertising. This long running series of advertisements historically involved one family's experiences over a dinner table and their reliance upon the simple stock cube. Oxo sold itself on its predictability. It is also easy to identify the marketing strategy and the audience the advertisers had in mind. The advertisement was aimed at 'housewives' seemingly responsible for buying such things as stock cubes. Therefore, a positive image of a household aided by the versatility of the product was consistently applied. The straightforward narrative of the advertisements adds to this notion of stability, as does the serialised nature of the campaign. Individually, there is relatively little to the adverts, but as a collective run, they sell a lifestyle as well as a product.

Typically, just when we think we have a straightforward strategy in the bag it changes and we have to start again. More recent Oxo adverts have steered clear from targeting the 'housewife' and are now aimed at other audiences. For example, a recent advert involves a young man making a stir-fry and commentating on his cooking as if it was a football match. This illustrates the ways in which advertisers are keen to keep up with societal trends and notions of feminine and masculine behaviour in order to maintain a mass appeal.

As mentioned, textual strategies change with societal technological and ideological developments. What textual analysis offers is a set of tools that can be applied to almost any moving image in order to best understand the ways in which they work, as shall now be demonstrated.

1.2 How to Read Texts

The reading or decoding of a moving image can be approached in the following way, which is useful when dealing with textual analysis in a classroom environment. The approach involves focusing on a number of specific technical factors (deconstructing the text) and then considering how they work together in order to make sense and meaning (reconstructing the text). The technical factors should hopefully function as a means of gaining knowledge about the meaning of a text, rather than just being features to spot.

The formal elements of film can be broken down using the following framework:

- Camera.
- Editing.
- Sound.
- Special effects.
- *Mise-en-scène.*

These offer a comprehensive overview of the ways in which a film is visually constructed as a text, and are a good starting point for what is essentially a structuralist analysis. Other dimensions can then be added to create new layers of complexity.

Camera (Cinematography)

This is the analysis of how the camera is manipulated in order to present the film-maker's visions of how things should look. It can have a number of desired effects. Here are some examples:

- **The long shot:** This shot shows a landscape or environment in an expansive way. As the term suggests, the frame captures a fair amount of space and is often used to establish a setting.
- **The extreme long shot:** This occurs when a camera captures an image from a distance, and is typically used to create a feeling of scope and magnitude, where a human figure may appear small. The archetypal extreme long shot is the famous scene in *Lawrence of Arabia* (1962), where the camera remains fixed as a rider approaches from a great distance over a long period. This is efficient in visually reinforcing the 'epic' tone and scope of the film.
- **The establishing shot:** This is used at the beginning of a sequence in order to provide the context of what

'This combination of both opportunity and angst accompanying today's media messages offers increasingly rich fields of exploration for students of the media, as well as those who study society. The two are inextricably intertwined. But the study of the media cannot be limited to an examination of the technology surrounding it and enabling it, although such a view is tempting. However, to look simply at the technical trappings is to look too simply at the world.'

Meta G. Carstarphen

we are about to see. Take news broadcasts – they generally begin with a wider shot of the presenter as a lead in to the headlines and top story.

- **The medium long shot:** This is achieved when a figure is captured almost in full, but where the feet and ankles are cropped at the bottom of the frame.
- **The mid shot:** This is when a figure is filmed from head to waist. This may be used when a character is to be seen doing something with their hands. For example, the infamous scene in *Taxi Driver* (1976) when Robert De Niro is seen talking to himself in a mirror uses a mid shot to capture the moment.
- **The close up:** This involves the camera focusing on an object or individual in order to draw attention to the filmed subject. When an actor is involved in a close up, an emotional impact can be heightened, simply because more emotion can be seen on the face of the character. Close ups are often used in soap operas, as they are an efficient way of conveying emotional reactions.
- **The big close up:** This is a head shot only, drawing attention to an important emotional response.
- **The extreme close up:** This is a close up from the eyebrow to below the mouth (or sometimes closer) which may be used to make a figure seem threatening. For example, in Ang Lee's *Hulk* (2003), extreme close ups are used to focus on Bruce Banner's face just before he transforms into the creature. This has the added effect of appearing like a panel of a comic book in this case.
- **The over the shoulder shot:** As the term implies, this involves positioning the camera over the shoulder of the subject and is also an effective way of creating tension.
- **Point of view shot (POV):** Here, the camera is meant to capture what a subject sees. If a sequence involves a burglar, the film-maker may give us his/her POV, accompanied with the sound of heavy breathing (is his/her face covered?) to increase the tension.
- **The angle of shot:** Depending on what angle a figure is captured at, the subject can be made to appear powerful (low angle shot) or inferior (high angle shot). Neutrality is created by shooting at eye level.

Hulk – *a close up shot conveys the menance and size of the furious superhero*

Camera Movement

- **Zoom (in and out):** This refers to when the camera focuses in or out of a subject. Zooming in can create tension, and zooming out can reveal something previously unseen. A simple way to see how a zoom in can attempt to create tension is to look at BBC2's *Mastermind*, where the camera slowly zooms in on the contestant as time elapses. An impressive example of zooming out to create scope can be seen in Peter Weir's **Master and Commander: The Far Side of the World** (2003), where Russell Crowe is filmed at the top of a mast, a zoom out shot revealing the insignificance of his ship against the magnitude of the ocean.
- **Tracking:** This is when a camera seems to follow a subject as they move. A good example of this is the famous long tracking scene in Martin Scorsese's **GoodFellas** (1990), where the camera follows Ray Liotta and Lorainne Bracco as they enter a restaurant. The effect of this can give the viewer an affinity with the filmed subject, as we are literally behind them.
- **Pan:** This is where the camera is turned or pivoted around an area, often to reveal more about it.
- **Whip pan:** A fast pan, usually used in an action sequence.

- **Arc:** This involves circling the subject with a camera, which can intensify their vulnerability.
- **Crane shot:** This involves a camera 'swooping' up or down from a subject. A good example of this is the closing frames of Terry Gilliam's *Twelve Monkeys* (1995), which ends with an impressive crane shot.
- **Steadicam:** This involves a cameraman harnessing a camera to their bodies using a specially engineered mechanical arm. This allows the camera to move at speed but remain smooth and is often used in action sequences to demonstrate velocity.
- **Aerial shot:** This is a shot from the air, usually when a camera is connected to a plane. The aerial shot is an effective means of conveying the scope of an environment, as seen many times in *The Lord of the Rings* (2001–3) trilogy. It can also be used in a more metaphoric and symbolic way. For example, in *American Beauty* (1999) an aerial shot opens and closes the film, conveying at first the mundane nature of the suburbs and later the protagonist's transcendence from them.
- **Hand-held camera:** This is used to convey a sense of documentary realism, as in *The Blair Witch Project* (1999). This can also be used to create immediacy and confusion, as in the opening scenes of *Saving Private Ryan*.

Editing (montage)

This is the way in which images are put together in order to retain coherence for narrative purposes, as well as create the tempo and tone of the text. Again, a number of techniques are employed during the editing process. These include:

- **Cuts:** This is when one image is followed by another without any noticeable transition. Some film-makers use many cuts, others use fewer. It may well be that certain film-makers attempt to create excitement by choosing to include many cuts. An example of a film with a large number of cuts is McG's *Charlie's Angels: Full Throttle* (2003). The director Michael Bay (*Bad Boys* (1995), *The Rock* (1996), etc.) rarely uses a shot that will run for more than five seconds. A film which uses relatively few cuts is Gus Van Sant's powerful *Elephant* (2003), which results in a sense of heightened 'hyper' realism. A high number of cuts can also traditionally be seen in the music video in order to convey excitement, and in musical cinema, as I shall discuss later.

- **Cross cutting:** This occurs when action is taking place at two or more settings at the same time. This can be a key feature of creating dramatic impact. A good filmic example of cross cutting is Steven Soderbergh's *Ocean's Eleven* (2001), where all the participants in a heist are cross cut together to create tension.
- **Reaction shots:** This is simply a shot of a person reacting to something that has been said or done. It is used to particular effect in horror films, where we see terrified reactions that set up enigmas as to what the characters are reacting to.
- **Montage sequences:** This involves different images being assembled to build up a sense of the characters and their relationship with each other. The montage is traditionally used in a title sequence. For example, *Hollyoaks* uses a montage in its titles. A filmic example of the montage takes place in the opening sequence of McG's *Charlie's Angels* (2000).
- **Flashback and flash-forward:** This is when a cut is designed to take us back or forward in time within a narrative in order to flesh out a story for dramatic or comedic purposes. There needs to be visual indicators that a flashback or forward is taking place. This has developed in complexity since the days of the mirage effect and the sound of a harp! Usually, realist drama and in particular soap operas, avoid flashbacks and forwards. (In the case of soap operas this may be because they are contrived to appear to be taking place in real time in the week of broadcast.)
- **Cross-dissolve:** A flashback may well include a cross-dissolve shot, where one image 'dissolves' into another. This is often used in the montage title sequence.
- **Fade in and fade out:** This involves an image fading in or out. Fading to black often tells us that time has passed and is used to end many films.

- **Multimedia:** This is when a number of types of moving image are put together. For example, real news footage may be put together with staged footage in order to create a sense of realism. Oliver Stone's **JFK** uses the infamous Zapruder footage of President John F. Kennedy's assassination to powerful effect. Other multimedia use could involve the marriage of CCTV and 'reconstructed' events in television shows such as *Crimewatch*. A recent development has been the incorporation of filmed 'cut scenes' in video games, which is intended to heighten the sense of realism for the players.

Sound

Sound is a crucial part of the editing process and a key way in which much of the narration of a text is conveyed. Before we see an image, sound can set tone and begin the narrative. For example before a single frame of Peter Jackson's **Lord of the Rings** trilogy is seen, the dramatic signature tune is played and the audience hears a voiceover; this sets a tone that is arguably maintained for the mammoth running time of all three instalments. Here are some of the ways in which sound is used:

- **Diegetic sound:** This is sound that the audience is meant to assume relates to the image and the action. So for example, if there is an image of a room with the sound of a phone ringing, we make the connection that the phone is in the room. Music can be used as diegetic sound also, for example when we hear songs played on the jukebox in the Queen Vic in *EastEnders* it is meant to be 'really' playing.
- **Non-diegetic sound:** This is sound that the audience knows is off screen and that characters aren't expected to be able to hear, such as incidental music or a voice-over.
- **Music:** The music used in a film is a vital component in creating the atmosphere and mood that the film-maker aspires to. The most striking examples of this have become iconic moments in cultural history. For example, the foreboding string bass in Steven Spielberg's **Jaws** (1975) is a part of cinema history. Similarly iconic in British TV history is the drumbeat at the end of an

episode of *EastEnders*. Music can convey dramatic tension, add to moments of action, and convey emotion and even terror. There are also recognisable generic conventions of music use, for example, rock music in action films, pop music in romantic comedies and the South American guitar sound associated with the Western. Specific songs may also be used in order to enhance sequences. This is used in some key films such as Francis Ford Coppola's **Apocalypse Now** (1979), which begins with The Doors' 'The End'. More recently, film-makers such as Quentin Tarantino and McG, have woven songs into films such as **Kill Bill** (2003–4) and **Charlie's Angels**, which are in some respects a montage of musical reference points. Some films have been described (usually pejoratively) as having 'MTV' influences, in that they have almost constant musical accompaniment making them resemble music videos.

- **Silence:** Silence can be used to add ambience or tension to a scene. For example, the US drama *Six Feet Under* often ends in silence to underscore an emotive moment, and fades out in silence to black.
- **Voice-over:** This can be seen throughout documentary film-making, and to link subjects in 'magazine' programmes such as the *Richard and Judy Show*. It can also be used for dramatic and narrative purposes as voice-over narration, as in **American Beauty** and **GoodFellas**. You may want to look at the original release version (1982) and Director's Cut of **Blade Runner** (1990), one of which has a voice-over and the other largely without, to see the effects that voice-overs can achieve.
- **Sound bridge:** This involves two scenes being interlinked by a piece of music. A good example of this can be seen in the sitcom *Friends*, where a recurrent set of short tunes links scenes. This may be accompanied by an exterior shot which tells us where the next scene is taking place (apartment building, coffee shop, etc.).
- **Title music:** The title music of a film is usually an original piece of music composed specifically for the film. A film's title music often encapsulates the tone of the film and is meant to emblemise the whole piece. This is also the case in television, where the style of

music is meant to befit the style of the show. For instance, the style of music used over the titles of *ER* is meant to embrace the dramatic nature of the programme. Replace that sequence with the title music of *Grange Hill* or *Will and Grace* and you have a very different thing indeed. Some television programmes use either an especially composed or an existing song that symbolises the show through lyrics. An example of the former is The Rembrandts' 'I'll Be There for You' as used in *Friends*; the latter, The Alabama 3's 'Woke Up This Morning' used in *The Sopranos*.

Special Effects

Special effects are of increasing importance with regards to the moving image, and in a constant state of technological development. But we must not assume that special effects are simply a recent phenomenon. Look at Merian C. Cooper and Ernest B. Schoedsack's **King Kong** (1933) or Victor Fleming's **The Wizard of Oz** (1939) and you will see that special effects have been with us a long time. We also must not see special effects as a purely cinematic phenomenon. Elaborate special effects are used increasingly in big budget television programmes. A recent episode of *ER* saw a helicopter fall from the sky and kill a regular character, and programmes such as *Buffy the Vampire Slayer* and the *Star Trek* franchise to some extent rely upon the advances in special effects and technology. Here are some of the many areas of special effects:

- **Miniature effects:** This involves the use of scale models. This used to be popularly used as a part of stop-motion photography as demonstrated by Harry Harryhausen. This can be seen in such films as **Jason and The Argonauts** (1963). Miniature effects can be seen in such films as **Independence Day** (1996) and **The Day After Tomorrow** (2004) where scale models of famous landmarks are destroyed. Stop-motion effects can also be seen in Aardman's Wallace and Gromit animations and **Chicken Run** (2000).
- **Stunts:** The oldest form of special effects, stunt work involves people performing physical feats under controlled circumstances. Some performers, such as Jackie Chan, have made careers out of their talent for combining stunt work with acting ability.

- **Pyrotechnics:** This involves the controlled use of explosives and fire in film. Used routinely in the action genre, it can be seen in spectacular form in *Apocalypse Now* in which helicopters strafe a Vietnamese village to the sound of Wagner's 'The Ride of the Valkyries'.
- **Motion control photography:** This involves filming miniature objects slowly using small cameras and then speeding the process up to create the illusion of size. This was developed by George Lucas's Industrial Light and Magic company for *Star Wars* (1977) and has since become widely used.
- **Morphing:** This involves taking two images and using a computer programme to meld one into another, the result looking like a process of transformation. This can be seen to great effect in James Cameron's *Terminator II: Judgement Day* (1991), where the T1000 can seemingly change from one person or object to another. Indeed, Cameron's *The Abyss* (1988) pioneered the process. In television, the vampires in *Buffy the Vampire Slayer* are seen to change by morphing effects. It can also be used to dramatically age a character, as in the end of *Saving Private Ryan*.
- **Make-up and costume:** These can simply dress a character and make them look a certain way, or can have far more significant purpose as in *Hellboy* (2004), where characters are made to look particularly unusual.
- **CGI (Computer Generated Imagery):** This involves a 'touching up' of film after principal photography, which can be minor or very extensive. A computer generates an image and imposes it upon the digitised image so that it appears to exist in the frame. The most accomplished example of this to date is the appearance of Gollum in *The Lord of The Rings* trilogy. In this instance a 'real' actor (Andy Serkis) was present throughout filming and acted the role on set. His movements were recorded by computer, which then 'mapped' Gollum into the scene. CGI is now a widely used phenomenon in cinema and is increasingly integrated into film. It is most clearly identifiable in action sequences, however it is also used in non-action orientated productions. For example, David Fincher uses CGI in *Panic Room* (2002) to allow his camera to

seemingly travel through walls, and it is often used in creating shadows to emphasise lighting effects.

- **Blue screen and green screen:** This involves filming actors against a coloured screen and adding background images during the editing process. Often used in fantasy, action and science fiction films such as *The Phantom Menace* (1999).
- **Wire removal:** A development pioneered in Eastern cinema, and used mainly in martial arts films. This involves using wires to allow actors to defy gravity, and then removing the wires in post-production (nowadays through the use of CGI). This has recently been seen to great effect in Ang Lee's *Crouching Tiger, Hidden Dragon* (2000).
- **Bullet time:** Pioneered during (and often parodied since) the filming of *The Matrix* (1998), this involves capturing a subject on film using multiple cameras at differing angles, the result being the ability to see the moving image from seemingly impossible angles. The effect of this is dizzying, in that the environment seems to move 'around' the subject.

Mise-en-scène

This is a term used to describe the formal organisation of images on a screen. The *mise-en-scène* is the way in which all of the above – lighting, camera, editing, and so on – work together in order to create the world the screen shows us. When we look at the screen we see all of these separate factors as one complete image – this is the *mise-en-scène*. Let's take an example of this in popular cinema that many students will be familiar with. In establishing Middle Earth for the filmed version of *The Lord of The Rings*, Peter Jackson must convince us (or at least persuade us to suspend our disbelief) that what we see is 'real'. In doing this he positions his actors in a certain way, he dresses them in a certain fashion, he uses special effects when necessary, he has the scene lit in a specific fashion, and so on. Another instructive instance of a sympathetic *mise-en-scène* is *The Girl with a Pearl Earring* (2003) where the film is cleverly styled to emulate the look of the paintings its protagonist (Johannes Vemeer) produces. Once a *mise-en-scène* is established, film-makers will wish to maintain its tone for reasons of continuity and quality. For example, one episode of *Holby City* will intentionally look and feel largely the same as another, both to establish a sense of 'realism' and to retain an audience attracted to the show's essential qualities.

Lighting and Colour

An aspect of *mise-en-scène*, lighting is used to create atmosphere and mood, often certain types of lighting are used specifically for certain genres:

- **High key:** Lighting that is generally bright and without a specific mood. This is often seen in the Hollywood romantic comedy and the Hollywood musical. Sitcoms and soaps often use this neutral lighting, as seen in *My Family* and *Hollyoaks*.
- **Low key:** This is darker and has far more shadows and contrast and can be seen to good effect in more atmospheric films such as the horror genre. Good examples of low key lighting include Ridley Scott's *Alien* (1979) and, more recently, *Hannibal* (2001). Television dramas may use this atmospheric lighting, as can be seen in the BBC's *Messiah* series.
- **Lighting from below:** This is used to make a subject appear threatening, as seen in *The Lord of The Rings: The Fellowship of the Ring*, in which Saruman (Christopher Lee) is filmed as an imposing figure.
- **Backlighting:** This often makes the subject appear sacred or mystical, as it creates a 'halo' effect. This can be seen in *The Lord of the Rings: The Two Towers*, where Gandalf returns, apparently from the dead, as Gandalf the White. It can also be used to create a silhouette, as beautifully achieved in Woody Allen's *Manhattan* (1979).
- **Colour:** Adding colour to a scene through lighting alters the palette and therefore the mood of the piece. For example, many science fiction films include blue and silver to represent technological coldness, as in Spielberg's *Minority Report* (2002). Warmer reds and browns are used in many Western films, and so on. If colour is rich and intense it is 'saturated' colour, as can be seen in *Moulin Rouge* (2001). Black and white can be used to show that a film is set in the past, as in Tim Burton's *Ed Wood* (1994). Sepia tones can add to the sense of the past as in *The Godfather* (1972). Sometimes colour is more explicitly manipulated. For example, *The Matrix*

trilogy uses sets, clothing and lighting all coloured a specific green, thematically referencing the green code that makes up the artificial world.

Character, Theme and Narrative

These key areas are not divorced from the formal structuralist analysis involved in looking at the above features, and should be taken into account wherever possible. The technical aspects of film are only of use if they add anything to the narrative of the film itself, and are best understood as working in conjunction with these crucial aspects of the text. For example, if an individual is backlit, surrounded by saturated colour and supported by dramatic music, we can be fairly sure that they have certain characteristics and are important to the narrative itself. The way in which a person is framed, lit, dressed and edited can hugely affect the audience response to them.

This is not simply an issue in fiction. For example, although maintaining an illusion of documentary realism, the reality television show is in part a product of manipulative film-making and invention. Take *I'm a Celebrity, Get Me Out of Here!* Contestants are often shocked by the seemingly unpredictable nature of the audience's voting habits where apparently charming, witty and engaging people are voted out in the early stages of the game, perhaps in part because the footage seen by the public has been edited in such a way as to portray the individual in a less than flattering light, or to diminish their role or influence within the group. On a reality TV show an innocent remark can be edited in such a way as to seem devious, a whisper can appear suspicious and a private letter can appear provocative.

1.3 Case Studies: The Action/Adventure Film

Action in film may feel like a recent cinematic phenomenon, considering the clichés we now associate with 'the action movie' or 'blockbuster' that are a regular part of the mainstream cinematic diet. However, action has been a key feature of cinematic practice since its conception. For example, one of the early landmarks of cinematic development is **Battleship Potemkin** (1925), which marked huge developments in film technique, particularly with regard to the concept of montage editing. Indeed, one of the most tension filled scenes ever constructed is in this film, the famous 'Odessa

Steps' sequence, during which a baby's pram rolls relentlessly down the steps in the midst of an assault on civilians by the Russian military. This scene is a template by which many of the elements of tension and action are built, and has been referenced, if not explicitly copied, in such films as *The Untouchables* (1987). As early as 1925 Fred Niblo provides an epic action sequence in the original *Ben Hur* (1925), and *King Kong* consists of all the elements of a spectacular effects-dominated film. Although directors such as George Lucas and Steven Spielberg are lauded (or vilified) as bringing in the dawn of the modern action spectacle, it is worth remembering that the *Star Wars* and Indiana Jones franchises are actually inspired by earlier adventure serials such as *Flash Gordon* (1936) – although this is not to discount the huge rise in the action/adventure film and the proliferation of action in the cinematic market post-*Star Wars*. Here are some ideas and terms applied to the genre:

- **The blockbuster:** This term was coined following the unprecedented commercial domination of two key films, *Star Wars* and *Jaws* (where queues of film-goers would line up for blocks around the cinema). The success of such films is often boosted by repeat viewings associated with a strong fan base and a, then, innovative pattern of theatrical exhibition whereby the film is opened 'wide', supported by extensive TV advertising. Now the term is used generically to describe a film (usually including a significant amount of action) that will cost, and potentially garner, a huge amount of money.
- **The popcorn movie:** this refers to a film that places fun, thrills and action at the forefront of the cinematic experience. Just as we may expect certain things from a film described as a 'chick flick' or a 'date movie', the popcorn movie is expected to deliver a significant amount of action. Recent examples of this type of film include *The Fantastic 4* (2005), *Charlie's Angels, xXx* (2002) and *Lara Croft: Tomb Raider* (2001).
- **The event movie:** This is much like the blockbuster, and may well be described as a popcorn movie, but is perhaps best distinguished by the products and promotions that surround the film itself. The event movie will have multiple franchise 'tie-ins', including deals with fast food multinational companies, toy makers, games manufacturers and various other

promotional outlets. These films are usually pitched to a younger audience, yet aim to have 'cross-over appeal' in that adults may appreciate them also. These are a part of a huge corporate machine, in which hype and market flooding are intertwined with the film-making process. The commercial viability of a film as a franchise is clearly considered for many action and adventure films. For example, the 'toyality' of a film is considered in the making of some productions. So the financial spin-off implications of a film such as **Spider-Man** or Tim Burton's **Planet of The Apes** remake (2001) become a major factor in whether or not the film will get the green light. Many have criticised this trend in film-making, and have pejoratively referred to it as the 'McDonaldsisation' of cinema.

- **The high concept film:** This is based upon an idea championed by the likes of Steven Spielberg that a really good idea for a film can ideally be summarised (or 'pitched') in a few sentences. A good example is Jan De Bont's **Speed** (1994). The pitch is: 'There's a bomb on a bus that will detonate if it travels below 50mph.' The high concept film is regarded by some as a contemporary phenomenon that has brought about a decline in the quality of popular cinema. However, I would draw attention to an earlier high concept film from 1933: 'Explorers capture a huge monkey and bring it back to the city, all goes terribly wrong.'

- **The set piece action sequence:** A set piece involves a build up of tension and usually a number of elements coming together in a climactic fashion. An action scene involves a high frequency of special effects and stunt work. There is a trend in many action films to include three or four action sequences and/or set pieces throughout a film, usually at its beginning, middle and end, with the final scene being the most spectacular. For example, Brian De Palma's **Mission: Impossible** (1996) includes a set piece followed by an action sequence in the first third of the narrative, a set piece in the mid section, and an action sequence at the end of the film. Interestingly, the final action scene was not included in the original draft of the script, but was added later to give the film balance and action credentials.

The Matrix Reloaded and the Action Sequence

The action sequence is a good opportunity to point out technical codes in (as it were) action, simply because it involves quite a lot of them in a relatively short sequential manner. They are also readily available, and can be related to the viewing habits of many students. Action sequences are very easy to spot, in that they rely upon spectacle, and usually (but not always, as Peter Jackson has proven) come in short digestible chunks. I wish to focus on the opening action sequence from *The Matrix Reloaded* (2003), and the ways in which the film-makers attempt to achieve their goals. Firstly, it is probably a good idea to anticipate what these goals might be, which is usually straightforward with regards to action/adventure films. Consider the following maxims of this sequence:

- It is designed to entertain an audience through spectacle, as should all good action films.
- As this is a sequel, the opening scene seeks to re-establish the world of *The Matrix*, which is particularly pertinent to this film.
- The sequence has a narrative function, in which events will dramatically affect the chosen characters.

The opening of the film stems directly from the opening title sequence (in this case sans titles), which is accompanied by non-diegetic music, familiar to the audience as coming from the first *Matrix* film. This is visually enhanced by the images of computer generated streams of binary codes, coloured in the 'matrix green', which runs throughout the franchise. This has the effect of reminding the audience of the premise of the film, which is that the world is a computer generated fiction rather than a 'real' place. Through spectacular digital manipulation, these binary codes are shown to be making up the fabric of 'real' things: a cog is shown then the arm of a

Clock/Code

clock, we then see this develop into the image of a clock on a wall as it strikes twelve. This has its own rhetorical impact in creating drama, and is aided by the sudden absence of music as it strikes. We then have an establishing shot, where security guards (as can be seen by their costumes) are shown changing shifts in what looks like a large, corporate building at

Security guards leave

night. We then quickly hear the roar of an engine

Trinity arrives

Trinity is revealed

(diegetic sound) before we see a leather clad figure fly from a rooftop, and summersault from a motorbike. This is presented in slow-motion using bullet time effects and accompanied by the recognisable dramatic score. The motorbike then smashes into the building and causes a huge explosion (created with pyrotechnics), which is also filmed in slow motion. The character then stands and removes their helmet, and is revealed with a headshot, as Trinity, a key character from the previous film. The *mise-en-scène* of this sequence places a familiar character in a familiar environment and a familiar predicament to those who have seen the first film. We cut quickly from an interior to exterior shot to create pace and tension, and the scene has been set. What has been established here relates to all three of the maxims proposed above:

- The sequence has involved the necessary spectacle, and has included stunt work, explosions and a crash, all cornerstones of the action genre.
- The world of the matrix is presented from the outset. This includes the characters, their costumes (the uniform blandness of the unwitting matrix slaves in contrast to the stylised beauty of Trinity), action, music and special effects.
- We see the character of Trinity attacking a corporate building. This has two narrative effects: firstly, it mirrors the opening of **The Matrix**, which also opens with Trinity. Secondly, this sequence is shortly revealed as a prophetic dream, and takes place in reality (albeit a computer generated one) as the film closes.

The sequence in question is both distinct to the style of **The Matrix** franchise and typically generic of the modern action sequence. By taking an example of an action sequence and asking students to examine the key features we identified on page 11, they can begin to explore the language of film in a genre in which this language can be clearly recognised.

These frameworks of analysis are by no means confined to investigating action and adventure films and sequences, which would obviously alienate a number of students and be limited in its scope. It may now be helpful to focus on another sequence, which also foregrounds a range of film-making techniques and is equally fast paced in a different way.

An Alternative Approach – *Moulin Rouge*

Although the action/adventure film can be a rich source that demonstrates many examples of film-making technique in an overt fashion, there is a danger that focusing on this genre can alienate certain students. This genre has been stereotypically associated with a young male audience. There have been recent attempts to include female leads in action films such as **Lara Croft: Tomb Raider** and **Charlie's Angels**, and using examples of these may be helpful. Alternatively, it could be argued that these films still appeal to a core male audience, with the female roles simply pandering to adolescent male fantasies. Using the action sequence as a starting point for studying the formal aspects of film is useful, but it is also helpful to be able to consider other approaches that clearly exhibit technique at work. For example, scenes involving sport exhibit many of the fast paced techniques as outlined above, as do dance sequences. The following is a shortlist of recent films that include these types of scenes:

- **Action:** *Van Helsing* (2004), *Crouching Tiger, Hidden Dragon, Brave Heart* (1995), *Die Hard* (1988).
- **Dance:** *A Knight's Tale* (2001), *Save the Last Dance* (2001), *Strictly Ballroom* (1992), *Dirty Dancing* (1987).
- **Sport:** *Seabiscuit* (2003), *Rollerball* (2002), *Any Given Sunday* (1999), *Raging Bull* (1980).

It may also be helpful to keep in mind the (albeit limited) examples of the action genre that are made by female film-makers (examples include Kathryn Bigelow's **Point Break** (1993) and Mimi Ledger's **Deep Impact** (1998)). A still more useful approach may be to find and use examples of film-making that utilise many of the techniques that can be seen so overtly in the action film, but working in a different context.

An excellent example of this is Baz Luhrmann's **Moulin Rouge**, which demonstrates a wide array of technical sophistication. The film is a veritable explosion of technique, and is one of the most overtly stylised cinematic examples of recent years. **Moulin Rouge** centres on a Parisian nightclub of the same name at the turn of the twentieth century, and concerns the love affair between a young poet and a burlesque courtesan, played respectively by Ewan McGregor and Nicole Kidman. The film is a postmodern revision of late nineteenth century Paris, full of contemporary pop cultural references and techniques which draw attention to itself as a film. Simply put, the film is about a time of excess and decadence, and therefore employs excessive and decadent film-making techniques.

I describe the film as 'postmodern' for the following two reasons, one concerning a visual and another a musical flair. Firstly, from the opening of the film, the audience is prompted to remain keenly aware of the façade of the film and the storytelling process. Before the narrative has even begun, this is made clear. The opening sound is that of an audience, with the first frame depicting a set of grand velvet curtains and a conductor. The curtain opens to reveal the famous 20th Century Fox logo and signature tune, which is conducted as though part of a performance. From the opening, then, the film *draws attention to* the process of film-making and performance. This can also be seen in the opening depiction of Paris, which is presented as if part of a silent, black and white picture. The film also draws attention to the process of narrative, as throughout the story the audience is made aware of the storytelling process. The story is narrated as a novel from the point of view of Christian (McGregor), and the audience sees him literally write the narrative throughout the rest of the film. The film also has what can be described as a postmodern approach to its musical content. Alongside music such as the Can-Can, which one would expect to find in such an environment, there are multiple uses of more contemporary music, ranging from performers such as Nirvana ('Smells Like Teen Spirit'), The Beatles ('All You Need is Love') and Dolly Parton ('I Will Always Love You'). The resulting film has a dreamlike quality and a camp sensibility, which mirrors the overtly stylised vision and romantic overtones.

Here I wish to focus on the first 20 minutes of the film, which in my opinion seeks to do two things:

1. To set the unique scene and tone of the film, needing to establish a world for the narrative to take place in.
2. To establish character and to set in train a plot that can sustain the audience's attention for the duration of the film.

The frameworks of analysis established earlier (camera, editing, etc.) are equally applicable here.

Camera

The camera is kept extremely busy throughout the film, especially early on, and this is in keeping with the fast paced, slightly insane lives the characters lead. With regards to the aims of the opening of the film, the camera can be seen to function in the following ways:

The figurative view of the Paris skyline

When presenting the city of Paris, the camera jerks through the streets, focusing on bizarre individuals that populate the surreal landscape. This has the effect of portraying a simultaneously familiar but strange environment. We recognise the stereotypical representations of gentlemen, whores and burlesque performers, as well as landmarks such as the Eiffel Tower, yet it is shot in such a way as to feel strange and unfamiliar, adding to the atmospheric tone of the piece. Extreme long shots of the Parisian skyline add to this – it is both familiar and yet clearly constructed and stylised.

Preacher outside Montmartre

Close ups are used to establish characters' emerging relationships to one another. The facial gestures become an important part of the opening scenes, portraying Christian's sorrow as he begins the story, his joy at entering the Parisian elite, and his desire for Satine (Kidman). Satine's ambition to become a 'real actress' is portrayed during a close up, as is her physical pain from her evident tuberculosis. This has a narrative effect; her inner feelings and potential demise raise the scenes' emotional register above the genre of the music video, and give notice of wider narrative implications.

Close-up of Christian and typewriter

Editing

The sense of the spectacular in **Moulin Rouge** owes a good deal to the editing. On a simple level, a frenetic pace is built up from the sheer speed of the cuts. In particular, the dance scenes are cut together at an incredible pace; usually a trademark of the action sequence as discussed earlier. There is also an extreme use of a zoom in and zoom out of Paris, which demonstrates the passing of time and

Dancers at the infamous Moulin Rouge

The flamboyant Zidler

establishes that the story is told retrospectively, adding to the sense of a loss of magical innocence.

There is a montage used near the opening that introduces the audience to the Moulin Rouge club and those who inhabit it. Its sense of notoriety and its scandalous reputation are established in this montage, and is made all the more effective by the incorporation of a voice-over to accompany the collected set of images.

Sound

As **Moulin Rouge** is a musical, the foregrounding of song is of course of paramount importance to the film-makers. Characters burst into song, emotions are conveyed through the types of music used, and there is barely a moment when both diegetic and non-diegetic sound are not evident. Indeed there is an interesting mix of the diegetic and non-diegetic in this and other musicals. Characters sing lyrics which are as significant to the plot as they are to making a musical play entitled 'Spectacular, Spectacular'. In this sense, this would be categorised as diegetic sound, in that the characters are supposed to be singing in the scene. However, in other circumstances (as when Christian bursts into 'The Sound of Music') orchestral accompaniment can be heard that is obviously non-diegetic. The result of this is that the sense of wonder that is produced with music is heightened, clearly reflecting the intention of creating a magical world.

With regards to character and plot, it is of course vital that emotions and characteristics are built up using songs that follow a narrative pattern. Lines within songs follow the mantra of the nineteenth century Paris, said to be 'truth, beauty, freedom, love'. Other sound effects are used to convey a sense of character as well as tone. The acting company that Christian joins is made up of idiosyncratic and bizarre characters. When they are introduced, sound effects from Warner Bros.' Loony Toons cartoons are used, reinforcing their absurdity.

Special Effects

The landscape of late nineteenth century Paris is clearly the result of special effects, especially miniatures, and there may be many digital effects used to create the spectacular vision. Colour is drained from some scenes, whereas in others highly saturated colour is used to foreground the excitement of the environment. There is the explicit use of digital effects to portray the hallucinatory effects of drinking absinth. Here the whole world turns the blue/green colour of the exotic drink, and the characters meet an absinth fairy (played by Kylie Minogue) before falling into a psychedelic vortex.

Stunt work is used to portray the characteristics of some of the characters and at one pivotal moment to present the verve of Harold Zidler (Jim Broadbent) who has seemingly superhuman energy, flying and back flipping across the dance floor despite his impressive girth. This adds to the sheer confidence and sense of daring that the character has, mirroring the flawed beauty of Paris as envisioned by director Luhrmann. Stunt work is also used when Satine falls from the swing where she is performing the climactic song of the first musical scene. This illustrates her vulnerability and acts as a metaphor for her demise later in the narrative.

Mise-en-scène

Moulin Rouge is a clear example of a film with a sustained and even excessive *mise-en-scène*; indeed some have criticised the film for being a purely visual rather than artistic endeavour, favouring style over substance. Certain films have memorable aesthetic principles that foreground the fantastic, and can be memorable for that very reason. Such examples include **The Wizard of Oz, Willy Wonka and the Chocolate Factory** (1971) and more recently **Amélie** (2001). **Moulin Rouge** also employs a remarkably colourful and incredibly busy palette to portray the stylised world of the film.

Zidler leading the 'Diamond Dogs'

Christian and his typewriter

Although the film is impressively colourful in the scenes in the nightclub, the exterior landscape is often colourless, dark and shabby. This has the effect of presenting the club as a shelter and escape from the outside world, where alcohol, music and dance act as a shield from the unwelcoming environment. In the scenes in the future, where the grief stricken Christian is writing the story, the environment is incredibly bleak, the contrast adding to the sense of the end of an era. The vibrancy of the club is therefore overshadowed by fears of illness, financial insecurity and the dangers of hedonism. This could be said to reflect the camp sensibility of the film. In her assessment of a camp sensibility, the writer and cultural commentator Susan Sontag has stated that:

> Camp is a certain mode of aestheticism. It is the way of seeing the world as an aesthetic phenomenon. That way, the way of

Camp, is not in terms of beauty, but in terms of the degree of artifice, of stylisation.

This assessment could be applied wholesale to **Moulin Rouge**, where the artifice and stylisation as seen in the *mise-en-scène* may well take precedence over depth of character. The artifice of this film is not intended to brush character aside, but to create a world where simple principles (beauty, truth, freedom, love) are a means by which a life can be lived.

Ideas

2.1 Genre and Narrative

Genre refers to the type of text in question, and can be approached in a number of ways. Firstly, there is a broad approach, which considers the medium under which a text is accessed. By this token, television and film are different genres. However, the sheer diversity of cultural output calls for cleared definition and categorisation. *Newsnight* and *The Osbournes* may belong to the same genre (television), but they are surely different enough to call for clearer definition.

Some TV genres seem to have been with us for a very long time, as in the soap opera, whereas some genres are newer to us, as in the reality game show. We also need at times to identify sub-genres, which provide us with clearer definitions. For example, *The Osbournes* and *Changing Rooms* are both examples of 'reality TV', but it may be helpful to further categorise *Changing Rooms* as a 'television makeover programme' and *The Osbournes* as a 'celebrity docu-soap'.

There are also clear examples of mixed genre hybrids, which take elements of two or more genres and combine them. For example, Ridley Scott's **Alien** is clearly a science fiction film as it is set in the future and involving space travel; yet it bears the hallmarks of a horror film, complete with monsters and gore, and it also includes elements of the action genre with its climactic ending. Another example is James Cameron's **Titanic** (1997). Is it a disaster movie, a romance or an action film? Some texts seem to defy definition, at least until we create a category for them to fall into. Take, for example, Richard Kelly's **Donnie Darko** (2001), a film about a troubled teenager coming to terms with among other things, time travel, a man-sized prophesising rabbit and his first girlfriend. Other examples include the films of the Coen brothers, who either clearly celebrate the clichés of a genre (as in **Miller's Crossing** (1990) and **Intolerable Cruelty** (2003)), or subvert genre definition (as in **Fargo** (1996) and **Barton Fink** (1991)).

Genre is a useful idea to keep in mind because a student's ability to define and discuss the workings of a particular genre show that they understand what is on screen and why it is being shown in such a way, even if they initially lack the proper vocabulary.

Identifiable generic codes can be seen on the following three levels:

- **The aesthetic level:** Certain genres follow aesthetic principles that define the tone and content of the texts. For example, film noir has a gritty aesthetic that befits the crime-ridden landscape it depicts. The Western also has a clear aesthetic design that remains to this day, as the recent film **Open Range** (2004) and the HBO series *Deadwood* exhibit. It is not only in film that aesthetic codes can be seen. Consider the glossy aesthetic of American crime dramas such as *CSI* and *Law and Order*, or the neutral aesthetic of most soap operas.
- **The narrative level:** Certain narrative trends can be identified, in accordance with the genre in question. For example, horror films often have a twist in the tale, adding to the shock value of the narrative. Most romantic comedies usually end with the two main characters becoming lovers. In television, there are also clear narrative trends. For example, the situation comedy is in part dependent on the very situation it depicts remaining roughly the same, with the same set of characters bound by their relationship to one another. Even non-fiction texts such as news bulletins and game shows follow clear narrative trends, as shall be discussed later.
- **The character level:** Certain character traits typify the players in certain genres. For example, the hard-bitten, cynical detective is a mainstay of much detective fiction, and can be seen from Mickey Spillane to Inspector Morse. The young female lead, terrorised by a psychopath, is a recurrent role in many horror films, from **Halloween** (1978) to **Scream** (1996).

Genre and Television

A good starting point for students involves the detection of recurrent tropes that help to define the genre of certain television programmes. In television, there are certain genres that for a long time have been the mainstay of the schedule. Consider the following examples:

- The game show.
- The soap opera.
- The situation comedy ('sitcom').
- The news bulletin.
- The crime drama.
- The talk show.

These models have spawned many incarnations of great diversity; yet have provided the basis for recurrent trends. Take, for example, the game show, which, although diverse, more often than not operates using the following schema:

- There is a regular presenter.
- Members of the public take part.
- The game is played in rounds.
- A winner is found by the end of the show.
- A prize is won.

Students can test the formula by coming up with ideas for their own game, and a key set of recurrent ideas is easily identifiable.

Other genres come into fashion at certain times, and may or may not stand the test of time. For example, in the late 1990s the airwaves were filled with cookery programmes such as *The Naked Chef* and *Two Fat Ladies* and although they remain popular at the time of writing (2004), their prominence has diminished somewhat. The same can be said for nostalgic programmes such as *I Love the 80s*, which peaked (perhaps unsurprisingly) just after the turn of the millennia. Currently the house-hunting programme and the auction show are popular, but we, the viewers, may well run out of interest in time. A major trend over the last decade has been the rise in reality TV shows, which has provided its own set of sub-genres (the reality game show, the celebrity endurance show, the makeover show) since its arrival.

There has, of course, been a healthy disregard for the conventions of genre from some quarters. Consider for example Channel 4's *Banzai*, which can be identified as a game show without requiring any of the generic trappings usually associated with the format. There are also many examples of cross genre television, as well as parodies of genre conventions. Consider the following examples:

The Office parodies the conventions of the fly on the wall documentary to considerable effect, melding it with the genre of the sitcom in order to breathe life into the format.

There have been some good examples of programmes that parody the talk show by creating a fictional presenter with the audience in on the joke. Mrs Merton, Alan Partridge and Ali G all work in the context of a talk show format whilst simultaneously undermining it.

Some programmes remain difficult to categorise into clear genres, indeed this may well be their appeal. For example, Channel 4's *Green Wing* is at once a situation comedy and a surreal sketch show.

We must also remember that new genres will come and go. Take for example, the current grisly trend in programmes depicting live footage of plastic surgery, or the upsurge in programmes based around auditions and celebrity hopefuls.

Although there have been parodies, and many examples of cross genre hybrids, do not assume that traditional genre is waning – it is alive and well. Take for example, the success of *My Family*, which firmly sticks to the generic conventions of the family orientated sit-com. The huge success of *The Weakest Link* and *Who Wants to Be a Millionaire?* should also be considered, as these are testaments to the durability of the general knowledge quiz show.

Codes and Conventions

This term or phrase is used to describe the recurrent identifiable patterns that exist in media and cultural texts. This can be everything from the technical aspects of film-making, to the ideological aspects of narrative and representation. Here are some examples of technical codes and conventions:

- **Lighting:** Situation comedies often use high key lighting, which adds to the overall lighthearted tone of the texts and possibly their unchallenging and unthreatening nature.
- **Sound:** Soap operas avoid non-diagetic sound within the narrative itself, which contributes to their 'realist' principles and tone. However, they do use music in key moments, usually at the end of the programme in order to heighten tension, as in the case of, for example, *EastEnders* ('dum, dum, dum dum', etc.).
- **Editing:** Action sequences in films are cut at a faster rate than other scenes, which creates the frenetic energy and the pace of the film.

We often take the codes and conventions of a form for granted, but it is the Film and Media Studies student's job to be able to identify, deconstruct and analyse them. It is perhaps best to begin some textual analysis on a limited scale and then build upon the practice. For example, one could begin with the analysis of a few trailers in a given genre (action/adventure, for instance) a music video (the boy band) and a type of advertisement (shampoo). Once some of these codes and conventions are established, students can begin to be more ambitious in their choice of texts, yet the principles will remain relatively similar. For example, an aspiring Film Studies undergraduate may write an impressive analysis of the representation of women in the films of Woody Allen. However they should be working on the same analytical principles of a GCSE student looking at the way in which women are presented in L'Oreal advertisements.

Narrative Theory

There are a number of key theories regarding narrative and a large body of critical work devoted to narratology. It has been suggested that the human mind has a propensity for organising events and information in a structured way as a means of making meaning out of the frenetic world in which we live. As such, narrative can be seen as a way in which all cultures relate to the world and events as they unfold. Film and television can be seen as one of the main outlets for the narratives that culture tells itself; and the organisation of these narratives into recognisable and often repeated structures is certainly a worthwhile thing for students to consider. Given our tendency to repeat certain narrative models in certain genres, narrative theory is closely linked to the study of genre itself. The narrative structure of the traditional Western film is a good starting point to consider. The story of a town under threat, saved by a group or individual outsider who rides into the sunset after a final conflict has provided many film-makers with a model to tell the Western tale. This is not confined to film: television sub-genres often follow recurrent narrative models. Consider:

- The final unveiling in a makeover show.
- The dramatic closure of a soap.
- The final round of a game show.

Often narrative structures are woven so deeply into the fabric of a programme that we can easily fail to spot them. Consider for example, soap operas or serials, in which the narrative begins in the morning and progresses as the day goes on until nightfall, as is often the case with *EastEnders* or *The OC*. At other times, narrative is so predominant to the modus operandi of a programme that it dominates the whole concept, as is the case with *24*.

Here are some key theories to consider.

Todorov's Theory of Equilibrium

The theorist Tzvetan Todorov focused on the structure of fictional narratives, where he identified a state of fragile equilibrium. According to his model, many narratives begin with a state of equilibrium, which is then disrupted by an event, forcing characters to face up to the disruption in order to reclaim equilibrium. Eventually, a state of equilibrium is restored, however the disequilibrium that has occurred may have left its mark.

Consider this model in relation to the following film narratives:

- **Jaws**.
- **Panic Room**.
- **The Lord of the Rings**.

The model is equally applicable to television narratives; indeed some genres *rely* on this format. Consider this model as applied to the following:

- *Star Trek*.
- *Spooks*.
- *Stargate*.

It has also been suggested that news bulletins are formatted in such a way that equilibrium is restored at the end of a bulletin where controllable normative issues (sport and weather) are focused in the final section of the programme. Todorov's theory may seem simplistic but does provide a basic narrative grammar that is surprisingly applicable to a whole range of media texts. But there is a tendency for students to over apply this theory, and it is undeniable that it is too general to apply to more complex narrative structures (as in **Fight Club** (1999)) or narratives where equilibrium isn't reached (as in **Resident Evil** (2002)).

Propp's Theory of Character Function

Vladimir Propp provided a model of narrative where characters and events can be seen as constructs, which exist in order to 'move along' and drive a narrative momentum. Using fairy tales as his basis, Propp identified a set of interchangeable character types that have clear functions in order to fuel a narrative. Some of these include:

- The hero, focused on a quest.
- The villain, hindering the hero on his/her quest.
- The donor, who gives the hero some magical key or information.
- The helper, who assists the hero on his/her quest.
- The heroine, who is used by the villain and is a reward for the hero.

In this model, the audience will identify with the hero and root for the successful completion of the quest, and therefore be opposed to the villain as hindering narrative closure and, thus, satisfaction. Because of its mythic origins, Propp's theory is most easily identified in fantasy based texts with mythic overtones. For example, some if not all of these elements can be seen in the film texts:

- **Star Wars**.
- **The Lord of the Rings**.
- **The Matrix**.

And in the following television texts:

- *Buffy the Vampire Slayer*.
- *Alias*.
- *Doctor Who*.

Although it is easier to apply Propp's theory to texts with mythic overtones, it can be seen in other, more realist texts. Consider the 'quest' faced by President Bartlett in *The West Wing*, or that faced by the eponymous heroine in **Erin Brockovich** (2000). A significant pitfall in Propp's theory is that students tend to apply it to every narrative and attempt to bend the roles played by characters in order to fit the model, leading to the misreading of certain narratives. What it is useful in providing is a means for students to begin to consider the text as a construct with characters acting as a part of a wider structure, and as such is a useful introduction to structuralism.

Lévi-Strauss and Binary Opposition

Claude Lévi-Strauss identified a narrative system of 'binary opposites' in which symbols and ideas exist in relation to their opposites, with which they are in conflict. The theory is that a simplified set of meanings is drawn from a text, where an idea is considered only in relation to its opposite, pandering to a viewer's need to side with a character who is 'good' against that which is 'evil'. Binary oppositions can be seen in the following:

Good	+	Evil
Male	+	Female
Us	+	Them

Following this model, we can consider the way in which many narratives are told from the point of view of the main protagonist, and consider what they 'are' in relation to what they 'are not'. For example, many Hollywood narratives are told from the point of view of a white, male figure, the hero of the narrative. This necessarily posits him in a privileged position inside the fold of the narrative, therefore, using Lévi-Strauss' model, we can identify what he exists in opposition to. The theory is interesting in that it draws attention to the fact that the world of a text is a constructed fiction, where simplified moral systems can operate (the grey area being removed).

Take for example, the traditional Western narrative, where the white, male, Christian, civilised cowboy battles against the non-white, pagan, savage Indian. In the simplified world of the fictional text, there are clear battle lines drawn between what is to be rooted for and what is not. Considering this, the logic behind feminist criticisms of the representations of gender in much of our culture can be understood, where strong, rational men exist as the natural opposite of weak, irrational women. Consider also, the criticisms aimed at **The Lord of the Rings**, where white, civilised heroes from the West battle black, uncivilised savages from the East.

Take the following examples:

- We can consider the simplified moral frameworks that exist in a programme such as *The West Wing*, which can be seen as either a ideologically driven piece of reductive propaganda, or as a coded attack on the degradation of values in the American political system.
- We can also look at the ways in which these binary oppositions have been destabilised in texts that explore moral ambiguity. For example programmes such as *The Sopranos* and *The Shield* create a world where notions of 'acceptable' and 'unacceptable' behaviour are redefined, in which the viewer is given the freedom to engage with the characters on a more complex moral level.

Narrative and Television

Narrative can be approached in a number of ways with regards to television. It is important for students to be aware of narrative beyond the boundaries of fictional plots, where a series of events usually unfold in a linear sequence. For example, an identifiable structure in almost any televisual form can be understood in terms of narrative. As such, a TV quiz show such as *The Weakest Link* has a narrative structure, with the stakes being raised as the contestants are gradually voted off the show. There is also a narrative climax at the final minutes of the quiz, with the possibility of, for instance, a sudden death situation, closing the narrative on a suitable conclusion. Even the evening weather forecast has a narrative structure in which information is arranged by the producers in order to be best received and understood by the viewers.

A good starting point in getting students to think in these terms involves investigating news broadcasts. Take, for example, the evening news broadcasts from the five terrestrial channels. Each involves an organised structure led by the main stories of the day, usually involving lighter hearted stories and sport at the end of the programme. In this respect they mirror newspapers, where sports coverage is placed in the final pages of the publication. This narrative structure is flexible, in that major news events such as the invasion of Iraq or the 11 September 2001 attacks can dominate an entire broadcast, and that on air events can be included as the programme occurs. However, an identifiable narrative organisation of events unfolds across the channels. We should also remember that the news is often organised on a macro level across the week. For example, there is sometimes more emphasis placed on domestic policy and inter-party debate on Wednesdays, when the Prime Minister's weekly Question Time occurs in Parliament. There is also naturally more time dedicated to sport on broadcasts at the weekend.

It is not just the linear organisation of information that works in terms of narrative. For example, a news item will be introduced by a 'lead' newsreader, who may be accompanied by another presenter who deals with another area such as sport. There will also be outside broadcasts from correspondents visiting news sites, (outside 10 Downing Street, at a sports ground, etc.) who relays information back to the studio in a pre-planned interview. There may well be the incorporation of in-studio debate, which can also involve outside links. Another recent trend involves audience participation in topical debates through technologically aided advancements. For example,

Channel 5 news includes text voting on news stories as well as the opinions of viewers via email and text. A large amount of time and effort is also dedicated to web based links with the main broadcasts. For example, Channel 4 often allows viewers to follow up on key stories by visiting their web site, where they can also air their views in web based debates.

From this we can see that almost any television broadcast involves a narrative organisation. *Ready, Steady, Cook* has its race against the clock and audience vote; *What Not to Wear* has the eventual revelatory makeover; and *Location, Location, Location* has the decision of to buy or not to buy. A useful task involves students looking at an example of a genre (game, makeover or property show, etc.) and identifying the narrative organisation of the programme. They can then choose a TV genre and come up with their own premise, which they can organise into three parts of a main narrative.

In terms of fiction, a number of narrative factors can be taken into account. For example, narrative can be approached in terms of individual characters and their storylines, in which the programme-makers focus particular attention on an individual. These can then be considered in terms of how they are organised in the wider narrative of a programme. A series of programmes will also have a wider narrative arc, in which storylines are developed over a much longer period. A number of series may be organised in terms of a macro-narrative, in which an overall story arc unfolds, often over a period of years. Take, for example, *The Sopranos*. *The Sopranos* focuses on the life of Tony Soprano, a Mafia boss in present day New Jersey. The narrative follows him and the lives of those around him, with each character having their own story arc, which develops as the series progresses. Consider the following organisation of the narrative at work here:

Each episode has its own narrative, in which a series of interconnected events occur which affect the characters. At times, individual episodes focus on key characters, where their own story in the saga progresses.

There are a number of broader story arcs that take place over a sequence of episodes, often being resolved over the course of a season. Such arcs have included the breakdown of the Sopranos' marriage, Tony's relationship with his therapist and Tony's cousin Christopher's battles with addiction.

Each season connects to the last, covering Tony's problems in managing his own life, his familial problems and the organisation of which he is head. There is a wider five-season narrative, in which all storylines exist in a sprawling saga in which some characters will live and others die.

The Sopranos is a programme focused upon the development of a main protagonist, focusing on Tony Soprano and his trials and tribulations. As such, once his story arc concludes, there is (one assumes) nowhere for the narrative to go.

Other programmes may well centre on characters, but have an ongoing longevity beyond the sum of its parts. Soap operas and serial dramas follow characters, yet live beyond the entrance and exits of individuals and families. For example, *Coronation Street* and *The Bill* involve characters that may have recurrent storylines over a period of years, and yet there isn't an unfolding narrative driven by a natural conclusion. It is conceivable, for example, that the creators of *The Sopranos* have always had an understanding of how the macro narrative will pan out. Indeed, they initially insisted that the show was only designed for four seasons, having since added a fifth. In contrast, we wouldn't expect the writers of *Coronation Street* to imagine the final episode of the soap (will there ever be one?) in which all the individual stories reach narrative conclusion.

2.2 Representation

It is important to notice that by providing a vision of the world on the screen, film- and programme-makers are giving us their version of events filtered through the creative imagination. There are painstaking lengths taken to manipulate and control what the audience actually sees, and film-makers have the power to move an audience in favour of one set of ideas or against another. Therefore, it is important that the ideology of texts remains under scrutiny, as they are sites of contestation and debate.

We must remember that in creating a text, film-makers are giving us a *version* of the world rather than the world as it really is. The audience sees a representation (re-presented on a screen) of reality rather than the unfettered truth. Once a moving image is produced and aired, it becomes a part of the cultural sphere, and is therefore a public document open to scrutiny. That is not to say that each text deliberately sets out to provide an ideological statement or that only texts that foreground ideologies are worthy of analysis. Moreover, those texts that may be happily unaware of their ideological implications may tell us a great deal about the culture that produces them. As the social climate of a culture changes, this is reflected in the cultural output and media representations. Consider a few sitcoms that have been popular in the UK over the last four decades and what they may or may not reveal about society and culture:

1970s – *Love Thy Neighbour.*
1980s – *The Young Ones.*
1990s – *Absolutely Fabulous.*
2000s – *The Office.*

The first thing to notice about these is that they could not necessarily be regarded as a definitive representation of 'what we were like' at any given point. For example, the 1970s was not entirely populated by rabid racists, nor the 1980s with anarchistic left-wingers; the 1990s was no more overrun with hedonistic socialites as the early 2000s was with unhinged paper merchants. However, they do exist as products of their time and their wider cultural relevance should not be dismissed out of hand as being 'just' sitcoms.

Mediation Theory

If considered in this way, one can identify interesting ideological undertones that reveal something about the state of our culture. It is also important to consider the ways in which the same thing can be represented in differing ways; such is the nature of subjective expression. Mediation theory focuses on the way we receive our view of the world increasingly through the media in the information age. Mediation theory takes as its premise the idea that we experience much of the world not from first hand experience, but through media outlets such as television and film. Take for example, the events of 11 September 2001: millions of us 'experienced' those events in a very real sense; however, we saw them through media institutions, rather than through first hand experience. As such, the events were mediated to us. Where mediation becomes interesting, is in the process of manipulation that can take place. Those that produce the images that we see (the mediators) have the ability to withhold certain information, and even the choice of creating an image that is altered for their own purposes. They have the ability to replace authentic reality for a manipulated hyperreality.

Here are some examples of differing representations of the same thing:

- The representation of New York. Most of us have a clear image in our minds concerning New York, in terms of geography as well as the type of people who live there. The image of New York that we have may come from our own visits to it, but may well come from our experiences of seeing it represented in cultural forms. However, which New York do we believe? Is it the glamorous New York of *Sex and the City* or the seedy New York of *The Sopranos*? Is it the New York of **Taxi Driver** (1976) or **Phone Booth** (2002)? Do we accept the New York of *Friends* – filmed in Los Angeles – or of **Eyes Wide Shut** (1999) – filmed in London?

• Consider also the representation of London. When we think of London as depicted on screen we can all think of wildly different versions. Which is closest to the 'truth' – the London of **Love Actually** (2003), *EastEnders* or **Dirty Pretty Things** (2002)? And how 'realistic' are any of them, really?

This notion is not restricted to fiction. A 2003 Thanksgiving visit to Iraq by President George W. Bush complete with roast turkey was revealed to be nothing more – literally – than a stage-managed photo-call: the celebratory bird was in fact made of rubber. This begs the question, how far can we rely upon news coverage? Politicians are acutely aware of how the image can be used to provide a version of reality...

There are two approaches to ideology and cultural texts that can be described in the following ways:

• **Texts reflect our ideology.** This relies upon the idea that the version of the world we see on the screen approximates our own world, complete with our own ideology and beliefs. This, of course, differs with the many versions of the world that are available to us! An example of this could perhaps be seen in the representation of gay and lesbian people in American sitcoms, the idea being 'we have become a more open society and this can be seen from our television'.

• **Texts influence our ideology.** This relies upon the idea that our beliefs and ideology are affected by what we see. To return to the inclusion of gay and lesbian in sitcoms, the idea would be, 'people will be less inclined to think homophobic thoughts after seeing such programmes'.

Of course, the way in which texts influence, and are influenced by, us is probably an amalgamation of these two ideas and will differ from person to person. The study into the representation of social groups has been at the forefront of Media and Cultural Studies since their inception, and there is a vast amount of theory and literature concerning the issue. It is widely accepted that the images and stereotypes that we see on our screens tell us something about dominant cultural values, and the ways in which these dominant cultures are challenged and affected over time.

Be it gender, sexuality, race, class, age, religion or any other social category, there is debate surrounding the ways in which the media portrays the individual. This relies upon the idea that when we see an individual portrayed on the screen, we are seeing a *type* of person (a representation) as well as the individual themselves. This is a difficult ocean for modern film- and programme makers to navigate and is a site of much debate.

For example, in 2001 Professor Jack Shaheen, published *Reel Bad Arabs*, a study into the portrayal of Arab and Muslim characters in cinema over the last century. Of the nine hundred or so films studied made by western nations, he found that almost without exception, Arab characters were portrayed in a negative light as villains and hate figures.

In considering this we must return to the two ways in which we can approach representation. That is, are these negative images the product of a racist society or do they create racism? It is not simply a case of negative representations, as students may be inclined to think. The media is in a constant state of flux and there are positive representations to counter negative stereotypes. For example, Shaheen points to recent films such as **Three Kings** (1999) as an example of films that include positive representations of Arab characters.

I now wish to give an account of some areas of study in the field of representation.

The Representation of Women

One of the foremost areas of study into the representation of social groups has been in the field of representation of women, which remains an interesting site of debate. Feminist theory has for many years scrutinised the media institutions and the ways in which women are portrayed on screen and in other media texts. Since the feminist movement has asserted its voice in the cultural sphere, the media has responded to this social change. The result has been the increased prominence of positive images of women in film and television in some quarters.

That is not to say this transition is as straightforward as it may seem. For example, film theorist James Monaco points out that in Hollywood films of the 1930s and 40s, women were often portrayed as intelligent and strong, with actors such as Katharine Hepburn representing the embodiment of these forceful individuals. There has also been significant development in key media genres. For example, crime dramas such as *Prime Suspect* feature strong female leads, which are exported throughout the world as syndicated shows. The sitcom has also seen the rise in prominent and positive representation of women, and all female cast shows such as *Sex and the City* are part of mainstream television culture. In film, the representation of women has been a central area of development in film theory. Key works have centred on the role of women in film as I shall discuss in Chapter 3 of this Guide. That is not to say that all problems concerning the representation of women have been overcome. Moreover, these positive representations only lead to more complex problems and issues of concern and texts such as *Sex in the City* are by no means a definitive solution.

The Representation of Sexuality

In 1985, Vito Russo published his groundbreaking study of the representation (or lack of representation in many cases) of homosexuality in Hollywood film entitled *The Celluloid Closet*. A massive undertaking, the book charts the images of gay men and women that infrequently turned up on the big screen over the twentieth century, and the stereotypical views that are highlighted and embodied in these representations. What is startlingly clear in this study is the sheer lack of gay and lesbian characters in mainstream cinema for decades and the ways in which Hollywood essentially eradicated all but a few manifestations of homosexuality in film. In the few instances where homosexuality was represented, the gay figure was all too often presented either as a tragic and doomed loner, often meeting his or her own death at the close of the film, or as a camp figure of ridicule and fun.

In recent years, there has been a more balanced approach to the representation of gay and lesbian people, reflecting the developing inclusive nature of parts of society. Some notable examples have been the representations of the PWA (Person With AIDS), one area where mainstream cinema has felt more comfortable in dealing with homosexuality. Examples of this include Jonathan Demme's

Philadelphia (1993), which includes the representation of a gay man with AIDS as played by Tom Hanks; and more recently Stephen Daldry's *The Hours* (2002), which includes the representation of a gay man with AIDS as played by Ed Harris. There have also been a few instances where gay characters (albeit secondary ones) have been represented outside the context of tragedy or farce, and have simply existed on film, as would any other character. Interesting examples of this include the character of Terry Crabtree played by Robert Downey Jnr. in Curtis Hanson's *Wonder Boys* (2000), and the character of Libby Holdon played by Kathy Bates in Mike Nichols' *Primary Colours* (1998).

Outside of 'mainstream' cinema, there have more often been representations of gay people that have generally been more positive and indeed interesting. On the small screen, there has also been significant developments in recent years which have led to more balanced representations of sexuality. The BBC television adaptation of Hanif Kureishi's *The Buddha of Suburbia* included the first aired gay love scene in 1992. In addition, in 1999 Channel 4's *Queer as Folk* was regarded as a benchmark in British broadcasting. *Queer as Folk* has also been exported and remade for American audiences. HBO's *Six Feet Under* has also been a significant development, not only because it features openly homosexual characters and themes as just another part of any (dysfunctional) American family. There have also been some interesting representations of gay people in soaps and sitcoms, which have a growing history of forefronting gay characters on a long-term basis. The kiss between Beth and Margaret in *Brookside* marked a change in what is considered a palatable issue for mainstream television, and it is now a trend to include gay characters as a central part of sitcoms. The most noticeable example of this is the popular *Will and Grace*, in which 'the situation' pivots around a gay man's relationship with a straight woman. It is interesting to note the comparative absence of lesbian representation in mainstream culture (outside the realms of period drama's such as *Tipping the Velvet*), as it seems we are currently more able only to (partially) integrate gay male culture into the respectable areas of the media.

The Representation of Race

The representation of race has been, and remains, a forum of much debate. There has been a long running debate about racial issues in all quarters of the media and the replicated image is no exception to this issue. As discussed, the versions of the world that we see convey a set of complex messages about ideology that media and film students seek to decode and understand, and the representation of race is an interesting area of analysis.

One good starting point is the historic lack of non-Caucasian people in UK and US cinema and television. Take for example, Hollywood cinema. The fact that there are key moments in Hollywood cinema where black characters are explored in a positive light (largely during the career of Sidney Poitier) serves only to draw attention to the lack of representation in most other mainstream cinema at the time. The same can be said of the 2002 Oscar ceremonies, heralded as a landmark moment of diversity in cinema because a black man (Denzel Washington) and a black woman (Halle Berry) won Best Actor and Actress awards. However, this draws attention to the shocking fact that in seventy-five years of the awards, only two other black actors had been successfully nominated.

The debate is not simply a historic one. For example in 2001 the French film *Amélie* drew criticism because of the version of Paris that was portrayed. Although the film was lauded as a success, the absence of any black characters or even extras in the streets of (in fact) racially diverse Paris was deemed offensive by some. Defenders of the film pointed out that the film is an expressionistic and fantastic vision of the city, however the version we see, exported throughout the world, remains problematic.

In British film and television, some of the multi-cultural aspects of society have slowly originated. Programmes such as the *The Kumars at Number 42* and films such as *East is East* (1999) show that Anglo-Asian characters and storylines can have a wide mainstream appeal. This can also be said for the incorporation of racially diverse characters in soap operas such as *Coronation Street* and *EastEnders*.

The Representation of Nationality

There are a number of ways in which nationality is represented in the media, and these can be indicative not only of the way we see ourselves, but also the ways in which we see others. The idea of a dominant culture, which sees that which is different as inherently 'other' and is therefore suspicious of it, is relevant in this context. It should also be remembered that within any nation, there are regional variations that have ramifications over what we consider as a nationality. For example, consider the representation of the English in film and television. There is a diverse and rich source of representations, which seek to portray a version of what it is and has been to be British. *East is East* and *The Football Factory* (2004) both offer a representation of British people, but neither can (or should) be taken as a definitive account of nationality. A way of approaching nationality and representation is to consider whether the text in question seeks to self-represent from within, or to represent from afar. For example, many nations have a notion of national cinema, that is, a cultural heritage of artists and even companies which foreground the production of texts that represent their respective nations. As such, there is a conception of Scottish cinema as being made up of film-makers and practitioners that foreground Scottish identity and issues in their work that is then exported throughout the world. Such films in this vein might include *Sweet Sixteen* (2002), *The Wicker Man* (1973) and *Orphans* (1997).

Some representations of nationality come from outside the culture in which a film is actually set. A good recent example of this is *Lost in Translation* (2003), an American film set in Japan which positions the western audience very much as outsiders looking into an apparently eccentric Japanese culture, rather than a Japanese film presenting itself to the world. This way of looking at the representation becomes complicated (and perhaps collapses) when a film is made specifically as an export providing a stereotypical and stylised view of a nation rather than a supposedly 'realistic' model. For example, Richard Curtis's vision of London as seen in *Four Weddings and a Funeral* (1994), *Notting Hill* (1999) and *Love Actually*, is (perhaps intentionally) very different from a 'realistic' representation of London: it is rather an idealised version that provides an international audience with a vision of English identity which emphasises such images as black cabs, Big Ben and Beefeaters.

2.3 Case Studies

Six Feet Under

Six Feet Under – *The Fisher brothers in a typically cheerful environment*

Six Feet Under is a highly praised series at the forefront of what is being heralded as a golden age of quality broadcasting from America. It is one of the flagship series from the Home Box Office (HBO) channel, hailed as the saviours of the American television industry. HBO has undergone a revolutionary transformation from a small independent cable television channel to a giant of the American television landscape.

Whereas it was once considered an outsider, it is now a mainstream competitor that often trounces massive rivals such as Fox TV and Paramount in the ratings war. HBO has a reputation for providing quality drama aimed at an adult audience, making such programmes as *The Sopranos* and *Deadwood*. These programmes are marked not only by their ratings success, but also because of their adult content, and willingness to extend the codes and conventions of each of their genres. What marks *Six Feet Under* apart even from these is the fact that it seems to defy genre definition. Based around a family of undertakers (the Fishers), the programme explores the ways in which each member of the family manages to negotiate their own grief after the death of the father, which takes place in the very first episode.

Six Feet Under is a hybrid of naturalist drama and expressionist film-making, including the incorporation of dream sequences and elements of fantasy as well as realist scenes and conversations. The success of *Six Feet Under* follows the success of **American Beauty** (1999), written by Alan Ball, the creator and producer of the programme. **American Beauty** is very much the creation that engenders the series, dealing as it does with a dysfunctional family in modern America.

Six Feet Under represents a shift from alternative film-making techniques into mainstream television, which began with the broadcast of David Lynch's *Twin Peaks* in 1991. *Six Feet Under* epitomises the sea change in attitudes towards television for the following reasons:

- Television is no longer considered as a less artful medium of expression than film.
- It involves aesthetic techniques previously attributed to film.
- It involves expressionism and experimentation.
- The time allowed to develop storylines and subplots over several episodes or an entire series is now considered a bonus lacking in mainstream cinema.
- Previously taboo language and sexually explicit scenes are included and bypass the certification system that dominates cinema.
- Whereas once television was considered a training ground for young film actors and a career dumping ground for older film actors, it is now considered a valuable creative mode.
- The expressionistic and experimental nature of the film-making in *Six Feet Under* is mirrored in the thematic issues and situations, some of which are explored for the first time in mainstream television.

Representation

At every turn, *Six Feet Under* seems to avoid stereotyping and explore the unexpected. Indeed this is at the core of the programme's popularity, in the sense that it is predictably unpredictable, and will avoid at all costs accusations of negative stereotyping. Here are some examples of representation in the series:

- **Gender –** The programme includes much sexual activity, yet attempts to avoid the stereotype of the predatory male and passive female. For example, one storyline is based around one female character (Brenda) suffering from sex addiction, jettisoning the notion that men are more sexually obsessed than women.
- **Age and sexuality –** One storyline focuses on an older woman (Ruth), apparently in the 'traditional' mould of home-maker and raiser of children, exploring her sexuality after a lifetime of marriage is brought to a violent end (the accidental death of Nathaniel Fisher upon which the events of the whole series are predicated). This has included an intense, ambiguous relationship with another woman and with a romantic crush bordering on obsession with a younger man.
- **Sexuality –** One of the main characters is a gay man (David) who during the course of the series has come out to his family and begun a relationship with another man (Keith). Crucially, their relationship, although by no means entirely stable, is the longest standing among the main characters.
- **Race and Sexuality –** The character of Keith is an openly gay African-American policeman (in the first season), encountering a range of stereotypes concerning gay men, race and occupation.

HBO is an example of an independent public access media institution, free from financial burdens in the large-scale media, which has superseded the mainstream. In doing so, it may itself have become embraced by the mainstream from which it once stood apart. The same can be said in part of *Six Feet Under*: its principles can be seen to lie in the alternative, both in terms of technique and theme, yet it is now a part of the mainstream culture which it may have once opposed or at least critiqued. It has been fully embraced by the establishment, as can be seen by the vast number of Emmy and Golden Globe nominations it has garnered. It will be interesting to see how cutting edge the series remains in relation to the new breed of programme that may follow it, commenting on and opposing the new mainstream.

Representation and Textual Analysis

Representation covers a wide variety of issues and social groups as discussed. But other than the over simplistic nomination of positive or negative representations of groups, it is at times difficult to pin down a systematic means of effectively approaching the subject.

The following is a simple way of approaching representation using three frameworks of analysis:

- *Mise-en-scène.*
- Editing.
- Narrative.

Mise-en-scène – concerning representation, students can focus here on two main questions:

- How is the image constructed?
- How does the character figure in the construction?

This focuses mainly on the visual representation of characters and the way they are positioned and filmed giving either an intended or subconscious meaning to the viewer. This can be either the ways in which an individual character is presented, or the ways that groups are presented *en masse*.

This could be a simple case of looking at the clothes a character is wearing (think of early Westerns where villains wear black and heroes white – which although largely outdated, still figures in such films as **The Lord of the Rings**). For example, is the clothing a character wears an indicator of a specific stereotype associated with a particular social group? We may also wish to look at the mannerisms that a character exhibits within the frame. For instance, does a female character act in a particularly 'feminine' way? And what does this tell us about their position within the wider text?

We can also consider the way in which a character is shot, framed and lit. A character can be made to appear menacing by being shot from below, being framed as a large figure in the centre of the screen, and lit from behind. It may also be that the character is presented as a desirable figure, caught by the voyeuristic gaze. For example, much has been written about the ways in which Alfred Hitchcock would position some of the women in his films as objects of desire, caught in the gaze of the camera. This has caused some to argue that this essentially objectifies women and reinforces a male dominated view of the word as discussed in Chapter 3 of this book.

Editing – Here, one must remember that a film is often edited in a certain way so as to privilege the point of view of one character and thus necessarily diminish the point of view of another. In other genres, we may privilege the point of view of one or more characters that make up a cast at different times. For example, a soap opera will involve an ensemble of characters, each with their own story arcs, who are each privileged at different points in the programme. This is a recurrent technique in sitcoms such as *Friends* and *The Office*, and dramas such as *The Bill* and *ER*. So, most programmes or films with ensemble casts are edited in such a way as to drop in and out of the point of view of the characters rather than film them all together all the time. There are of course exceptions to this: recently *The Royle Family* took the step of mainly filming all the characters in unison to much acclaim; and Hitchcock's **Rope** (1948) is assembled in such a way as to suggest the film is made of one continuous shot. Many films, however, involve one main character or set of characters that are the focus for substantial periods. They are, therefore, no only an important part of the *mise-en-scène*, but also the way in which we receive their reactions to situations, the amount of close up or head shots they receive, and the way the camera is positioned in relation to them becomes crucial. Think again of a Western. In a shootout the camera is often placed below and behind the protagonist – we are behind them, literally.

The use of voice-over is also of importance with regards to privileging a point of view. Usually, when we hear a voice-over we have a natural desire to side with the protagonist who is speaking to us. Just as we would automatically seek to sympathise with the narrator of a novel, we have the same desire to sympathise with what is essentially the narrator of the film. As with literary fiction though, this narrator may not always be reliable, as can be seen in such films as **The Usual Suspects** (1995).

A good example of the utilisation of voice-over can be seen in Martin Scorsese's **GoodFellas**. In one sequence the main character Henry Hill (Ray Liotta) describes the first date he has with his future wife, Karen (Lorraine Bracco), which does not go well. Up until this point in the film, we have seen the world almost entirely from the point of view of Henry in a narrative that is centred on his life story. Much of this centrality is achieved by the use of voice-over, which is extremely prominent in the film, adding to the sense of autobiographical authenticity that it seeks to achieve.

During the couple's first date, which Henry has been talked into by his friend Tommy (Joe Pesci), Henry's voice-over tells us that he couldn't wait to leave as we see him rush through his dinner.

Suddenly, we then get the voice of the Karen, telling us how rude and arrogant she felt he was acting. At this point, another voice (and, therefore, point of view) is added to the film, and Karen goes from being a minor (and mute) character to being a fully formed individual. In the next sequence we learn that she is a Jewish American, adding a layer of complexity and depth to a film that has up until this point been inhabited almost solely by Italian Americans. As the two then become a couple, we follow their next date in an impressive and justly famous four minute tracking shot of them entering a busy nightclub via the kitchen. This dazzling shot communicates the sense of them as a romantic item as we follow them through the labyrinth out onto the floor of the supper club. This air of romance is reinforced by the soundtrack as the The Crystals' 'Then He Kissed Me' is playing (with Scorsese's typical flair) as non-diegetic sound.

Concerning representation, this sequence has a number of effects. Firstly, it adds a female perspective to a narrative that would otherwise be almost entirely told from a male point of view. The audience is given a representation of the mobster's wife, complete with all the moral complexities of benefiting from a husband's life of crime. The audience also attains an insight into the issue of marriage between ethnically diverse individuals in American culture. We must also remember that Bracco and Liotta are representing real people (the film is based on a memoir by the real Henry Hill, mobster), and the inclusion of both voices further adds to the sense of authenticity.

Narrative – Narrative is one of the main ways in which characters and their characteristics are relayed to us. In a sense, narrative dominates and affects other aspects of film such as editing. For example, if a film centres on the story of a particular character, it needs to be filmed and edited in such a way as to privilege their point of view. Therefore, the other characters in the film that the protagonist sees in a favourable light may well be shot and edited as to appear in a favourable light and so forth. If we continue our Western analogy, if a film concerns (narrates) the figure of a cowboy fighting against American Indians, they may be portrayed (represented) in a negative light, as is the case with many early to mid-twentieth century Westerns. However, the film may follow the story from the point of view of Native Americans exploited and oppressed by white settlers, in which it is they who are portrayed positively and the white oppressors who are shown in a negative capacity.

Class and Nationality in *Sweet Sixteen*

Ken Loach's *Sweet Sixteen* is another film in the oeuvre of the director that deals with individuals marginalised by mainstream society. Other such films include **Raining Stones** (1993), **Ladybird Ladybird** (1994) and **My Name Is Joe** (1998). The film is set in the Greenock area of Glasgow, and depicts a grim vision of a deprived urban estate. The text is a quintessential example of 'gritty social-realist drama' that Loach has specialised in throughout his career, and focuses on elements of society that are rarely depicted in commercial cinema. *Sweet Sixteen* centres upon a boy named Liam (Martin Compson), a fifteen year old deserted by his father whose mother is in prison for drug related offences. Liam begins the film selling smuggled cigarettes in the pubs of Glasgow, and after stealing the heroin stash of his mother's boyfriend, Stan, becomes a heroin dealer. The narrative follows him as he becomes drawn into the criminal underworld and ends with him stabbing Stan to death after he tries to stop his mother returning to him.

Although *Sweet Sixteen* essentially concerns a criminal who deals heroin and ends the film as a killer, the protagonist is a sympathetic figure trying to survive in a society that leaves little other opportunity for him.

Mise-en-scène – What is striking about the *mise-en-scène* of *Sweet Sixteen* is the thoroughly mundane tone of the visuals. The film is almost universally visually bleak, reflecting the hopelessness of the situations the characters live in. The palette that Loach chooses is made up of muted greys, and this is retained throughout the entire piece. Loach has also chosen to set large parts of the film outdoors, emphasising the imposing grimness of the concrete sprawl of the area. This is broken with occasional visits to the coast, which come at crucial times when Liam is in need of escape. He dreams of buying a caravan on the coast and escaping the estate on which he has been raised, and visits it whilst planning his emancipation. The flat that is

Liam cuts through the urban sprawl

provided to him by a crime boss in return for his services is also on the coast, representing again the possibility of escape. As the film ends Liam is on the run after the stabbing, and ends up on a beach. This is a possible route out of his desperate situation, but also, perhaps, a potential place for him to commit suicide. There is a contrast then: between the

The coast acts as a metaphor for escape

concrete landscape that the characters feel trapped within, and the natural landscape that offers potential escape.

Although overwhelmingly bleak at times, the film also has moments of aesthetic beauty, which offset the grimness of the environment. The film opens with Liam selling views of the night sky through his telescope to eager children, and we see stars in the sky, which represent the dreams of the young (drawing perhaps, from the infamous Oscar Wilde quip 'We are all lying in the gutter, but some of us are gazing at the stars').

Editing – A number of identifiable editing and camera techniques are employed, which reinforce the intention of the film. For example, at key moments, a hand-held camera is used in interior setting, which gives the film a 'jerky' quality, adding to the realist aesthetic principles of Loach's vision. At other times, wide angle shots show the expanse of the bleak landscape, which seems to stretch for miles. The effects of these two techniques used in tandem are as follows. In close quarters there is a jarring sense of instability, used to particular effect during some of the violent scenes and when characters joyride in stolen cars. In exterior shots, the grey landscape seems to bear down on Liam, and he seems overwhelmed by his surroundings. The overall result of this is the expression of pressure that the main character is feeling, which builds as the film progresses.

Another aspect of the editing process is the sheer amount of screen time dedicated to the main protagonist. The film is edited in such a way as to privilege the perspective of Liam, resulting in empathy between viewer and character. True, we see him participate in criminal acts that would usually be attributed to unsympathetic characters; however, this is juxtaposed with images that endear him to the viewer. For example, at one point Liam participates in an initiation ceremony into a gang in which he agrees to kill a man who he has never met. We see him rush towards the man to kill him, before the gang members rush to stop him, revealing that the assassination is simply a test of loyalty. This scene is then juxtaposed with an image of him shaving for the first time, reminding the viewer of the age of the boy and the more personal initiations into manhood he is going through.

The way the film is shot also adds to the way an audience will respond to the character. For example, just as Liam is at the centre of the film and inhabits almost every frame, he is also the only character to be filmed in close up, where emotional reaction and response is revealed. The result of this is that, although he looks like a 'typical' working class petty criminal (the colloquial term being 'ned' in Glasgow), we see the boy behind the stereotypical exterior. We also literally see through the eyes of Liam at some points. He has an interest in astronomy and owns several telescopes. At points he looks through a telescope in order to survey the activities of other drug dealers in the area. On these occasions his point of view is filmed and we see what he sees, again putting the viewer in a position that encourages empathy with the boy.

Sound is also edited into the film at key points in order to develop emotional and poetic aspects of the character and his predicament. At one point, Liam and his best friend Pinball (William Ruane) steal a car and are joyriding. The music the car owner has on his stereo is operatic, and the two play it whilst performing hand break turns. Although the music is essentially diegetic, in that it comes from the car stereo, it is used in the same way as non-diegetic sound. In the exterior shots of the car, the music is still heard, the allusion being that the car is 'dancing' to the music, and the characters are joyriding to escape their otherwise mundane existences.

At another point, Liam is making a tape recorded message to his imprisoned mother. At the end of his message, he records The Pretenders' 'I'll Stand By You', which is then kept on the audio track as we see Liam sell drugs on the street. Here, diegetic sound mutates into non-diegetic sound, and the lyrics of the song underline his loyalty to his mother. So, although we see him participate in criminal activity, the fact that he is doing so in order to save money to buy himself and his mother a home is brought to the forefront and his position as a sympathetic character rather than a caricature of a Glaswegian criminal is strengthened.

Narrative – As discussed, *Sweet Sixteen* very much centres on the main protagonist, as can be seen by the amount of screen time devoted to him. In terms of narrative, the film is Liam's story, and his journey into the criminal underworld provides the main narrative thrust of the plot. The film seeks to go beneath the stereotypical representation of a criminal and social dropout and offer some insight into the motivation for his anti-social behaviour. However, it is also a representation of the Glaswegian estate where it takes place, and this aspect of the narrative should not be ignored. For example, Liam's increasing reliance upon criminal activity as a source of income is not unique, and his story can be seen as a familiar one to many. On another level, the issue of hard drug culture in deprived areas of

Scotland is also brought to the forefront, and the social problems depicted can be seen as having a wider contemporary relevance.

The contemporary social relevance of the film is heightened by Loach's social realist film-making principles. As discussed, the *mise-en-scène* of **Sweet Sixteen** is one of gritty realism, and this can be seen in other elements of the film such as the performances and the dialogue. Most of the actors in the film are relatively unknown, and provide extremely naturalistic performances throughout. Crucially, Compton and Ruane, the two actors playing the leads, are newcomers, and deliver performances that seem unscripted and spontaneous, adding to the sense of the film as a social document rather than a purely dramatic piece. The dialogue is also of interest, with all of the characters speaking in extremely broad Glaswegian accents which again adds to the sense of strict realism.

Although **Sweet Sixteen** is stylistically presented in almost documentary format, there are elements of classic drama that are recognisable. The narrative can be viewed in the context of a modern tragedy, with the central character forced into violent and tragic action because of forces that are beyond his control. Liam is doomed from within, with his dogged determination an asset that drives him to change his life, and the thing that draws him into the violent underworld. He is also doomed because of his situation, essentially abandoned by his parents and lost to the school system. With regards to tragedy, it is also pertinant that Liam almost escapes his situation at points in the narrative, only to have all his hopes crash around him as it closes. The film also follows the classic gangster narrative as seen in many films depicting the experiences of those in the Mafia. Liam's increasing involvement in the criminal underworld and his initiation into a gang may be familiar to anyone who has seen such films as **GoodFellas** or **The Godfather**, however the stylistic differences make this a very different type of film. The romanticism and stylistic violence are replaced with a heightened sense of realism that refuses to see crime as anything other than a product of society.

Another important aspect of the narrative is the fact that it remains open-ended as the film closes. After stabbing his mother's boyfriend, Liam flees from the scene to the coast, which has up until this point been symbolic of potential change and escape. The closing shots of the film see him wandering aimlessly along a beach, now wanted by the police for his crimes. The film ends without letting the audience know the outcome and the viewer is left to imagine a potential future or demise for the protagonist. This open-ended narrative works in an extrapolative manner, in that the viewer is engaged with thinking about the film beyond the boundaries of the plot itself, and encouraged to consider wider ranging contexts and social problems. Loach refuses to offer the audience a satisfying end to the narrative, which could limit the scope of the film as simply another tale of a descent into crime, and thus encourages an active viewer who will work to provide their own possible outcomes.

Critical
Approaches

Media and film theory is a vast body of work encompassing a huge amount of writing from a diverse range of thinkers. Film theory is practically an industry in itself, as a proliferation of publications hits the shelves on an almost weekly basis. Film theory is now a widely recognised concept, just as film is a widely recognised art form. However, the concept of 'film as art' has not always been the case, and in its genesis, film theory sought to legitimise the genre of film as worthy of real intellectual attention. In this chapter I wish to provide a brief survey and description of some of the major theories around film which are applicable to the post-sixteen learner. This survey will by no means be exhaustive and will only offer an overview and perhaps a route of further research. It is intended solely as a taste of the rich and complexly diverse theoretical *oeuvre* available. Section 3.1 is best considered as a range of critical approaches that can be disseminated and relayed to students in an understandable fashion. Section 3.2 deals with how these approaches can be put into practice with students and uses case studies of the Steven Soderbergh film **Erin Brockovich** and the TV comedy drama *Shameless* to illustrate this.

3.1 Schools of Thought

There are key schools of thought that can be applied as critical approaches to film. It must be remembered that one of these schools of thought, structuralism (also known as formalism), forms the basis for the entire first chapter of this book, which aims to show ways in which the structure of film can be deconstructed and understood. The key areas of interest in film theory are:

- Structuralism.
- Psychoanalysis.
- Postmodernism.
- Auteur Theory.

- Feminism.
- Queer Theory.
- Marxism.

Psychoanalysis and Film

Film has been used to provide a representation of mental states since its infancy, be it through character action and expression, dialogue, or the expressionistic formulation of dream-like states. Some film-makers have identified the potential of film to reproduce dreams and other imagined settings. Surrealist film-makers such as Luis Buñuel and Salvador Dali have committed their visionary and bizarre images to celluloid in such films as **Un Chien Andalou** (1929). Other film-makers (for instance, Terry Gilliam, Tim Burton and David Lynch) include surreal visual imagery in their films as a part of a stylistic aesthetic.

Some film-makers have been interested in (or have later been credited with) exploring deep psychological dilemmas and issues of the human mind as identified by the likes of Freud and Jung. For example, it is widely accepted that some of the films of Alfred Hitchcock (for instance, **Marnie** (1964) and **Psycho**) explore the Oedipal complex as suggested by Freud.

In the 1970s, film and cultural critics such as Christian Metz and Umberto Eco added to this by considering the way in which we use cinema in society (so the cinema is an apparatus of society), and the way in which an audience member is positioned and urged to react in a certain way. These theorists saw editing (montage) as a series of manipulating gestures that aim to engage a viewer response. With this, the film-maker produces images with the idea of a viewer in mind, and therefore promotes a set of values with this imagined audience member in mind. Therefore, a viewer who fails to identify with these values, or who consciously rejects them, may feel alienated from the process. This predominantly psychoanalytical view of film has been criticised as too narrow an approach to deal with the vast arena of cinema: however, it has dramatically changed the ways in which film study is approached. More recently, psychoanalysis of film has been used as part of an arsenal of ways to approach film, and is a valuable tool in such areas as queer theory.

Here are three ways to approach psychoanalysis in film; each is more difficult than the last for the purposes of differentiation:

Level 1 — The mind-set of characters

Students can identify and consider the psychological state of a character or set of characters within a film. For example, if we take the example of a film such as **American Beauty** we can see it is about the emotional and mental state of a set of characters, so the emotional journey of the main protagonist fuels the narrative. A film can also represent the emotional and mental temperature of a society or community. For example, films such as **Minority Report** or **Enemy of the State** (1998) portray paranoid societies where individuals experience tension because of this climate.

Level 2 — Symbolism

Students can identify the way images, props and sounds are invested with a symbolic meaning, which can then be read or interpreted by the viewer. For example, in the film **Angel Heart** (1987) Robert De Niro plays the human embodiment of the devil ('Louis Cipher'); at one point in the film he sits talking to the main protagonist, Harry Angel (Mickey Rourke), while peeling a hard-boiled egg, which he then devours with relish. As we later learn, 'Cipher' has possession of Angel's soul, and so retrospectively, the egg becomes symbolic of the soul. Another example is the 'Director's Cut' of **Blade Runner**, where Deckard's dream image of the unicorn symbolises freedom from the oppressive world that the characters inhabit. Symbolism involves images working on a denotative and connotative level, and includes signs being read as symbols as discussed in Chapter 1 of this Guide.

Level 3 — The subject position of the audience

Here, we can ask students to consider the ways in which an audience member is made to potentially feel an emotional empathy for some characters, whilst feeling alienated towards others. Do we follow a character and see things through their eyes? Are they placed before us as objects of desire, or as figures of fun? We can also identify the way the viewer is positioned in relation to an image. For example, is a subject filmed in such a way as to titillate? If so, does this potentially alienate those who are excluded from this exchange? Are certain characters or characteristics positioned as 'other' (that is, different from a received norm), and if so what does this tell us about the values of the film-makers and the perceived values of the audience? A good starting point here is Laura Mulvey's seminal essay 'Visual Pleasure and Narrative Cinema' (1975), which includes an interesting investigation into some of Hitchcock's films, among others.

Psychoanalysis in Television

Similar principles can be applied to television as with film. However, TV provides its own interesting representations of psychological states that lend themselves well to the genre. For example, the very nature of television allows for an at times detailed exploration of psychological states, with far more screen time devoted to relevant issues over a longer period of time. Be it the unstable psyche of Yosser Hughes in *Boys from the Blackstuff*, Tony Soprano's long-term battle with anxiety in *The Sopranos*, or the struggle of the Fishers to deal with grief in *Six Feet Under*, a great deal of TV screen time has and continues to be devoted to psychological states.

These explorations are not confined to serious drama: consider, for example, representations of agoraphobia in *Shameless*, and of paranoia and self-obsession in *Seinfield*. Soap operas have also provided long-term depictions of mental and psychological illness and conditions, often spanning years at a time. Consider, for example, the ongoing mental problems faced by the character of Jimmy Corkhill in *Brookside*, or the depiction of alcoholism in characters such as Phil Mitchell in *EastEnders*.

Some dramas, and in particular the genre of psychological crime drama, have explicitly put psychological analysis at the forefront of their project. The long running drama *Cracker* makes much gripping drama out of the psychoanalytical prowess of its protagonist, as well as his own battles with alcoholism true to the form of detective fiction. More recently, ITV's *Wire in the Blood* is a study into the mental states of serial killers, focusing on the analytical dexterity of Dr Tony Hill.

There has also been valuable representation of real people living with psychological challenges in the field of documentary. It is doubtless that many viewers' understanding of psychological states have been affected by documentaries which seek to provide a serious and in depth exploration of psychological challenges, and to counter reductive stereotypes of mental illnesses and other challenges.

It is also worth considering the subject position of the TV viewer, distinctly different from the cinemagoer, with the constant flow of TV into the living room. Consider for example, the long-term bonds that can be developed between a character and audience member in a long running drama or soap opera. Viewers can experience a deeply felt loss after a soap character is killed off or retired, a result of the prevalent role of the characters in the viewer's life not least because of the repetitive and addictive nature of the production. Television is scheduled round our lives: consider the desperate viewer asking around for a recorded VHS copy of *24*, distressed after missing their weekly fix of the addictive show.

Postmodernism

Postmodernism is a difficult concept to relay to students, simply because the term encompasses so many ideas that are themselves often oblique. The idea of postmodernism encompasses architecture, literature, art, film, politics, economics and much more. It can even be considered as a mode of living or coping ('the postmodern condition') in the capitalist, information age. Whereas modernist film-making laments the rise of mass production as a threat that can dehumanise the individual subject (as seen in films such as **Modern Times** (1936) and **Metropolis** (1927)), postmodernist film-making celebrates the artificial veneer of mass production (perhaps as a form of critique) and popular culture, and seeks to identify and celebrate inner depths in the outwardly shallow. I will now cover some of the key concepts of postmodernism and specifically relate this to film using a variety of examples.

Bricolage

This involves a playful and often ironic mixing of different genres, modes of film-making and 'high' and 'low' artistic aesthetics. A film-maker will feel free to cross borders that govern formal genres, codes and conventions and techniques in order to create a text that is both fractured and yet inherently recognisable. For example, Baz Luhrmann's **Romeo and Juliet** (1996) is at once both recognisable as the Shakespearian play, and yet borrows from a vast array of sources (gangster films, pop music, culture and costume, for example) in order to seek a fresh approach to the well-worn narrative. It abandons the notion of realism in a strict sense and yet abides to it at other times in order remain intact yet fundamentally dichotomous. Another example of bricolage can be seen in Quentin Tarantino's **Kill Bill: Vol. I** (2003), where Japanese-style animation (*animé*) is integrated into a live action film.

Meta-reference

This involves a film-maker drawing attention to the act of film-making and fiction within the work. The film will employ a meta-fictional technique of letting the audience know essentially what the illusion of cinema is. An example of this the Spike Jonze/Charlie Kaufman film **Adaptation** (2002), where the main character, named 'Charlie Kaufman', is desperately attempting to write a follow up to a hit movie, mirroring Kaufman's own position after writing **Being John Malkovich** (1999). Another example of self-referential film-making is **American Splendour** (2004) in which the actor (Paul Giametti) playing the 'real life' protagonist, Harvey Pekar, is filmed watching him between sections of the film.

Intertextual reference

This involves film-makers making specific references to other popular cultural forms and other films. Film-makers such as Quentin Tarantino and those influenced by his success have most popularly utilised this technique. This can be clearly seen in the opening scene of **Reservoir Dogs** (1992), in which characters discuss the subtext of Madonna's 'Like a Virgin'. Tarantino's intertextuality reaches new heights in both **Kill Bill** films, which use intertextual reference as their basis. For example, the *mise-en-scène* exists almost entirely in homage to other films, mainly made up of the genres of martial arts and the Western, as well as a large amount of references to other works by Tarantino. For instance, the yellow and black costume worn by The Bride, played by Uma Thurman, is based upon the one worn by Bruce Lee in **Game of Death** (1978). Another of the many examples includes the fact that the car driven by Bill (David Carradine) is the same model as driven by the actor in **Death Race 2000** (1975). References to other Tarantino films include the pose struck by Budd (Michael Madson) in the door of his trailer mirroring that struck by the actor in the infamous torture scene in **Reservoir Dogs**.

Narrative

Postmodern theory has involved the rejection of so called 'grand narratives', that is, a unified social history that is widely accepted as genuine and authentic. It is no surprise then, that postmodern film has questioned, deconstructed and reconstructed versions of narrative conventions. This can be seen in a number of ways, as follows:

- **Non-linear forms:** Postmodern films challenge the received wisdom and use of the linear three act narrative structure that we see in so many films, and offer new approaches and alternatives to this convention. Film-makers such as Quentin Tarantino disrupt the linear action of their films and sequence the work in such a way as to explore different points of view. For example, in **Pulp Fiction** (1994) the final part of the film returns to the point at which the film opens. The result of this is that the sense of a fixed unified narrative is disrupted, and a singular point of view disappears. Therefore, we see a set of individuals inhabiting the cityscape, rather than a coherent worldview from a main character.

- **Stories within stories:** Some films employ the postmodern technique of including sub narrative forms within the body of the main narrative, another self-referential technique drawing attention to the artificial nature of the medium. For example, *Scream 2* (1997) begins at a screening of a film (screech) within the film which echoes the events of the first *Scream* (1996). This is made all the more complicated by the fact that the first *Scream* film can barely be called 'the original' as it consists of a pastiche of pre-existing films and genre codes. Add to this the later existence of *Scary Movie* (2000), a satire of a satirical pastiche, and the complex issue of postmodern culture becomes apparent, if no clearer.

- **Simulation:** Much has been written about the ways in which we increasingly use reproduced images and ideas (simulacra) in our culture. The postmodern theorist (e.g. Jean Baudrillard) would draw attention to the fact that we seem to function on a *simulated* rather than *authentic* aesthetic plane. In this respect, a T-shirt reprint or a mouse mat version of Van Gough's 'Sunflowers' is a postmodern image, in that it reproduces art out of context for different purposes. Often the original context of an image can be lost: for example, the simulacra of the image of Che Guevara has more relevance now as a icon of the fashion world rather than its original photographed manifestation. It may be that film lends itself extremely well to the idea of postmodernism, in that it overtly and consciously tends to re-create and simulate a version of reality rather than reality itself. This simulated reality can also be seen in such films as *Moulin Rouge* or *Amélie*, which consciously draw attention to the artificial nature of the presented environment as a constructed set.

This is not to suggest that this conscious creation of hyperrealism is a recent development. Consider, for example, **The Wizard of Oz**, which can retrospectively be seen as including many of the hallmarks of what could be considered as a postmodern aesthetic. This simulated reality can also be seen in the trends of reproduction that occur in the film industry. Postmodern theorists point out that in the modern world, the idea of authorship comes under scrutiny and strain. For example, Van Gough can be on one level seen as the author of the original 'Sunflowers'; however can he be considered the author the T-shirt or mouse mat which follows? This has a particular relevance to film. Although the original 'Sunflowers' exists and is valued in the material sense, in that a source painting exists which has been touched by the brush of the artist, film is not produced in this way. A film is meant to be reproduced as a print, rather than an original with copies made from it. In a sense, a film only really exists as a film (rather than a piece of celluloid or a digital image) after it has been premiered and essentially handed over to the public. This idea has become complicated by the existence of 'Directors' Cuts' and 'Special Editions', which depart from the original theatrical releases, so we are left wondering where the original lies.

Postmodernism and Television

Television provides us with some key postmodern texts and trends, and may well be suited to the idea because of it populist credentials. For example, Chris Morris's *Brass Eye* and *The Day Today* take the format of the television news report and reconfigure it as a social comment using a postmodern approach to intertextuality. Intertextuality can also be seen across a broad range of television text in a number of ways. For example, *Arrested Development*, a programme concerning the breakdown of the modern nuclear family, contains a voice-over narration by Ron Howard, involved in part because of his involvement in *Happy Days*, an ironic nod to the very different Cunningham family of which he was an onscreen member. Other shows have celebrity guests in a postmodern reference to the construction of the text itself. For example, the use of celebrity guests in programmes such as *Friends* and *Will and Grace* invites the audience to share in the knowledge that what they are seeing is a construction made for their own entertainment. Perhaps the most intertextual programme of all time, *The Simpsons*, is awash with references to pop culture, some of which are obscure and some more clearly identifiable.

Television can also illuminate the mass media's desire to take individuals and images from their original contexts and re-invest them in a new situation. For example, *The Osbournes*, in which the original source of fame is eclipsed by the protagonists' involvement in a soap/reality TV documentary. Surely one of the most jarring examples of the postmodern ethos is the rise in programmes that take celebrity figures and recast them in bizarre challenges for our 'entertainment': the sight of former Sex Pistol John Lydon covered in bird food locked in a pen with ostriches on *I'm a Celebrity, Get Me Out of Here!* was one many of us never expected to see.

Auteur Theory

During the first half of the twentieth century, the film-making process was considered a collaborative enterprise between many individuals. Indeed, Hollywood prided itself for much of this period on the studio system that worked as a film-making factory and could produce films at an incredibly rapid rate. At the end of the 1940s, a new theory arrived from France, from the pages of *Cahiers du Cinéma*, which essentially identified and championed authorship (hence *auteur*) in cinema. In 1948, the film critic Alexander Astruc contended that the control that a film-maker asserts over the camera was comparable to a writer's control of the pen, where the author manipulates and directs the reader through skilful means. In 1954, critic and film-maker François Truffaut identified a group of directors as 'auteurs'. These directors not only asserted a clear aesthetic sensibility to their films, but also a thematic strand that occurs throughout a body of work. Originally applied to established directors outside of the Hollywood system such as Ingmar Bergman and Akira Kurosawa, the term legitimised those it was applied to as authentic artists working within a serious art form. A significant development occurred when European proponents began to turn their attention to Hollywood film-makers such as Alfred Hitchcock and Howard Hawks, lauding them as artists working within the confines of a studio system.

The term has been widely used to describe not only the film-makers of the French New Wave (some of whom, such as Truffaut and Jean Luc-Godard, pioneered the concept as critics), but also those involved in the New Hollywood of the 1970s such as Martin Scorsese, Francis Ford Coppola and Robert Altman. Since then the term has been clearly overused, and applied as a plaudit to almost any who direct a few well received films with an aesthetic quality. One of the results of this overuse has been the devaluing of the currency of the term and hence a distrust of the concept itself.

Auteur theory remains a debatable issue, and the concept has certainly been overused to flatter certain film-makers. It may be that it imposes a romantic vision of the artist on to the director, detracting from the skill and artistry of writers and cinematographers. There is also the question of the amount of input a director has. For example, it is fairly easy to credit Woody Allen as an auteur, as he writes, directs, acts in and helps edit films which have recurrent themes within them. However, what of Steven Spielberg, who helms projects that are massive in scale, involving a range of aesthetic approaches and themes that are not obviously recurrent? Film studios have also appropriated the concept of the auteur for the purposes of marketing. By assigning artistic authorship to a film (i.e. 'a film by Ron Howard', or 'a Ridley Scott film'), they make the idea of authorship a part of the currency of the contemporary film business. It is the auteur theorist's emphasis on the individual artist, rather than the creative team, which many have called into question. Although widely ignored by psychoanalysts, feminists and postmodernists, there has recently been a resurgent interest in the theory from some neo-formalists, who identify an artistic presence in the formal organisation of the film.

Auteur Theory and Television

For many years, the concept of the auteur was only applied to film, revealing of the lack of artistic credentials attributed to TV and typical of an implicit critical hierarchy between the two media. More recently, the idea of the television auteur has become less remote, and as part of a revisionist strategy, we are looking back and re-examining creative forces in television.

For example, we can now look back at the comedy writing duo of Dick Clement and Ian La Frenais (*The Likely Lads, Porridge,* etc.), and identify the work of artists within the medium. Others stood out in their own time, and staked a claim for genuine artistry on the small screen, and can be seen as televisual auteurs. Two towering examples in British television include Alan Bennet, whose *Talking Heads* is viewed as a masterpiece best fitted to the form of television; and Dennis Potter whose work (including *Pennies from Heaven, The Singing Detective*) is remembered as among television's best.

Auteurism can be considered in the following ways with regards to television:

- **Authored work:** Certain writers are credited with having an artistic vision that drives television into the realm of art, and are held up as the authors of important works. For example, writers such as Lynda La Plante (*Prime Suspect*), Jimmy McGovern (*Cracker*) and Paul Abbot (*Clocking Off*) are all seen as skilled writers of television who can launch projects with their own name attached to it. Interestingly, the accolades afforded to writers of television are rarely given to the writers of films, where the director is often credited as the true creative force. Other writers are valued as the creators of programmes, even though they may not write or even conceive of every plot, character or storyline. For example, Michael Crichton is regarded as the creator of *ER*, Steven Spielberg as the creator of *Band of Brothers*, and Matt Groening as the force behind *The Simpsons*.

- **The film-makers:** Certain individuals can be seen as providing an aesthetic and thematic artistic vision to the television they make. This can come from a number of sources. Firstly, there may be the case where a recognised film-maker turns to television after establishing a voice in cinema. For example, David Lynch originated, and directed some episodes of, *Twin Peaks*, and Mike Nichols has increasingly worked in TV, most recently with *Angels in America*. Sometimes this may occur only in one episode, as when Quentin Tarantino directed an episode of *ER*. In the second case, certain film-makers have established an ongoing creative presence in television, as is the case with Stephen Poliakoff (*Shooting the Past, The Lost Prince,* etc.).

- **The studios:** At times, the creative kudos a television programme has can be seen as coming from the organisation that produces it. For example, the HBO channel is seen as a creative hot house where talent and art are garnered and produced, resulting in the likes of *Sex and the City, Six Feet Under, The Sopranos* and *Deadwood*. In the UK, certain presumptions are made of our own broadcasters and their strengths. For example, an adaptation of a Jane Austin novel from the BBC may be seen as having serious creative potential, while ITV has specialised in the production of such crime related successes as *Prime Suspect, Cracker* and *Trial and Retribution*.

Feminist Film Theory

As feminism provides a critique of ways in which women are expected to act and are treated in society, it is perhaps logical that feminism turns its attention to the ways in which women act and are treated in the media, which seeks to portray a version of society. Feminist film theory is a fruitful and diverse area that has had a serious impact on film theory as a whole, and has provided many with a useful way of approaching film. Although primarily focusing on gender, feminist film theory also provides the analytical tools by which other significant areas (for instance class, race, and nationality) are available for exploration. For the purposes of this Guide, feminist film theory can be considered as mainly covering the following.

Representation

It would be a mistake to impose a simple progressive narrative concerning film history that begins with the presentation of women as weak willed and dim in early cinema and strong and intelligent in contemporary cinema. It is worth noting that characters portrayed by actresses such as Katharine Hepburn during the 1930s and 40s were often strong, competitive and fiercely intelligent. However, it is clear that many stereotypes have been historically reinforced by filmic representations of women. The dizzy blonde was virtually perfected by the likes of Marilyn Monroe, and the vengeful vamp epitomised by Glenn Close in *Fatal Attraction* (1987). What may be considered on the one level as a generally more positive representation should also come under scrutiny on another. For example, films such as *Alien*, *Terminator 2* (1991), *Thelma and Louise* (1991) and more recently *Erin Brockovich*, have all been lauded as 'feminist' in some way or form. However, this does not position them above criticism. For example, the female action star may be a male fantasy played out on the big screen, with attitude and anger replacing other stereotypes. It is also notable that the aforementioned films are produced and directed by men in an industry that is male dominated. Whatever the developments, feminist film criticism has brought the issue of representation to the forefront of media and film discourse, resulting in a more acute awareness of our cultural ideology.

The Male Gaze

This concept stemmed from the 1970s when feminists began to consider the ways in which film-makers positioned the viewer in relation to the characters within the film. Retrospectively analysing films from the likes of Douglas Sirk and Alfred Hitchcock, theorists such as Laura Mulvey (1975) concluded that the camera was positioned and manipulated in such a way in these films as to privilege the point of view of the male viewer, who is able to voyeuristically gain visual pleasure from viewing the female subject. It has also been contended that film-makers such as Hitchcock objectified his female subjects, positioning them in such a way as to offer titillation.

From this the violence towards women in such films as **Psycho** can be read as revealing a deep-seated misogyny towards women with violent and disturbing undertones. This formative body of theory has led to an upsurge in ideas concerning the ways in which male and female viewers receive cinema and the positions from which subjects are captured on film. What the theory is perhaps most successful in achieving is taking close analysis of montage and editing, and combining this with a psychoanalytical approach to film.

Women and film-making

Laura Mulvey ends her pivotal analysis of the male gaze by ascertaining that avant-garde approaches to film-making have the potential to subvert traditional film-making conventions and create a new radical cinema that can be used for the purposes of feminism. There has also been some interesting research in the genre of 'The Woman's Film' both as a means of reductive representation and as a potentially revealing and oppositional expression. 'The Woman's Film' is a genre traditionally made for and marketed to a female audience, and can be most notably seen in the melodramas of the 50s and 60s, and recently in the straight to video/DVD market. These films are usually domestic dramas centred around family life, and deal with so called 'women's issues' such as family break-ups, romance and pregnancy. These films have been criticised by some as pandering to stereotypes and being intellectually lightweight. However, others have argued that within the constraints of the genre, women's roles within the family, and forms of oppression are potentially explored in these films. There has also been much discussion concerning female actors, stars, directors and practitioners in the industry as a whole, and the ways in which the film-making business can act as a microcosm of wider social dilemmas.

Feminism and Television

There continues to exist a robust and interesting debate concerning gender in television, which is a rich source of study for a student of the media. Television has the ability to stir up public debate around such issues because of its mass popularity, and continues to divide and certainly engender much opinion. Consider a few examples that have seemingly galvanised public debate if not harmonious agreement.

The Life and Loves of a She Devil gripped the nation when it was screened in 1986, and the story of a downtrodden woman's transformation into a vengeful and fearsome matriarch was seen by many as an allegorical transformation from the domesticated servant into the competitive 80s businesswoman. Other stories of the wrath of the downtrodden female have gained massive attention. *The Politician's Wife*, the revenge tale of a forgotten woman's divisive but brilliant plot to turn the tables on her husband took up the mantle of the She Devil; and the media coverage brought about by Little Mo's eventual reaction against her abusive husband, Trevor, in *EastEnders* was enormous.

The issue of representation has also stirred up debate within different factions of the feminist movement with liberal feminists arguing that changing representations will result in altering public opinion, and more radical feminists arguing that negative representations are a result of public opinion. On the subject of representation, the following genres are a good starting point for discussion:

- Crime drama.
- Soap opera.
- Sitcom.

The crime drama has been a genre where much change has occurred, reflecting and perhaps changing some social values. This is optimised in *Prime Suspect* where the gender of DCI Tennison is of little consequence to her intellectual capacity, yet important to the struggles she faces as a career-driven woman. From this, there has been a wealth of television drama inhabited by strong and interesting female characters, including Amanda Burton's portrayal of Dr Sam Ryan in *Silent Witness* and recently Caroline Quentin's portrayal of DCI Janine Lewis in *Blue Murder*.

Soap operas are of interest not least for the fact that they depict domesticity and are inherently domestic themselves, scheduled around the routines of the 'typical' family day. There is a long tradition of hardship among women in soap operas, resulting in variations and explorations of women's role in the community.

Sitcom has been an area where changing social values and causes concerning women and accepted 'feminine' behaviour have been brought to the forefront and used for the purposes of comedy. Some sitcoms have dealt overtly with the issue of feminism by depicting young women breaking out of the domesticated roles expected of them and exploring their own independence. In Britain this can be seen in *The Liver Birds*, and in the US there was *Laverne and Shirley*. This trend can also be seen in the phenomenon of *Sex and the City*, which centred on the experiences of career women and the redrawn lines of gendered behaviour. This has also affected the representation of masculinity in sitcoms. For example, the sitcom *Men Behaving Badly*, where the politically incorrect behaviour of the main characters is humorous precisely because it falls short of the 'new man' sensitivity that exists in the context of feminism.

It is not only in fiction that we see change and the debate it incorporates. These can be seen across the landscape of television. Consider, for example, the role of women in the news, as both presenters and correspondents, and the ways in which this has mirrored changing attitudes and values. There have also been some recent interesting developments in new television genres. For example, the property ladder genre, which has boomed over the last few years. There has been a proliferation of female presenters in this genre, valued for their domestic knowledge of house surveying and good business acumen, rather than their ability to cook and clean.

Representations remain a fierce area of debate. For example, to some, *Sex and the City* may appear to be a landmark series speaking out to the modern western women facing similar dilemmas, whereas to others it is just another set of stereotypes, perpetuating impossible beauty standards and reductive values. Equally, for some *What Not to Wear* may be a programme that celebrates women of all ages and sizes taking control of their body image and lives, whereas to others it is another example of objectification which sees women view themselves only through the eyes of others.

Queer Theory

The term 'queer' is used to describe an area of theory that foregrounds gay, lesbian and bisexual issues in culture. The word has been re-appropriated as a positive symbol of gay rights and empowerment and is used in an affirmative context. The lesbian and gay liberation movement has been a significant force in media and film theory for some time, and developed into queer theory as an organised academic presence in the 1990s. Just as feminism privileges the discourse of gender and power in society, queer theory takes approaches to texts and textual production in the light of sexuality and alternatives to heterosexual 'norms'. As such, it shares much in common with feminist theory. For example, a psychoanalytical framework is often applied to textual analysis, as is a critical assessment of a received heterosexual ontology. Both also consider the notion of 'othering' in cultural production and reception: that is, representations of alternatives to patriarchal heterosexual dominance that are read as negative, abnormal or disruptive.

The following areas can be seen as covering different but interconnected areas of queer theory.

Queer readings and history

This involves taking a somewhat revisionist approach to film history and considering the presence (and, crucially, *lack* of presence) of alternative sexualities in film. A good starting point for this is Vitto Russo's *The Celluloid Closet*, which provides a comprehensive survey of the first eighty years of Hollywood's treatment of homosexuality. Queer readings can also be applied retrospectively to films. For example, a queer reading of **The Wizard of Oz** would not only consider the aesthetic issues and the camp sensibility of the film, but also the perceived difference of the characters and the allegoric significance of this.

Queer reading can also be applied to contemporary cinema. For example, the aesthetic principles and thematic concerns of Baz Luhrmann (as seen in **Strictly Ballroom** (1992), **Romeo and Juliet** and **Moulin Rouge**) can be approached and arguably best understood from a queer perspective (regardless of the sexuality of the director himself).

Lesbian and gay film-making

This takes into account the works of gay and lesbian film-makers working in an overtly queer context throughout history, as seen in the careers of, for example, Derek Jarman, Kenneth Anger and John Waters. It also considers the work of others dealing with the issue of difference in a more metaphoric sense, as seen in some of the work of Dirk Bogarde. It considers the work of contemporary lesbian and gay film-makers such as Todd Haynes, Pedro Almodovar, Donna Deitch and Ana Kokkinos, and the ongoing affects of a queer presence in cinema.

Camp

This is both an aesthetic and thematic aspect of cinema and refers also to wider visual forms and cultural practice. Camp aesthetics celebrate the overtly artificial and make beautiful that which is flawed and 'false', as can be seen in the entire concept of drag and performance. Camp films include everything from the loud, brash and overtly queer, as in the films of John Waters, or a text such as *The Rocky Horror Picture Show* (1975), to the more subtle aesthetic qualities in the work of Douglas Sirk (e.g. *All that Heaven Allows* (1955), *Imitation of Life* (1959)) and modern revisions of it in such texts as *Far From Heaven* (2002). Camp themes also find beauty in the tragically flawed, and camp characters are often defiant in the face of adversity. So, the characters played by Bette Midler (as seen in *Beaches* (1988), for instance) can be understood as exhibiting a camp sensibility celebrated by some members of the gay community.

Queer Theory and Television

A good starting point in approaching the issue of homosexuality and lesbianism in television is to take into account the sheer lack of gay characters in mainstream television throughout its history. The fact that we can point to 'landmark' representations of gay characters in television demonstrates this disparity in historic terms. Nevertheless, the history of gay representation in television is a history of firsts, be it the first openly gay character in soaps or dramas, the first gay storyline, or the first gay kiss. Headlines have been made by such things, and scenes from *The Buddha of Suburbia, Brookside* and *Coronation Street* have all made the news. Other programmes have dealt with the issue on a more overt level. In British television, John Hurt's portrayal of Quentin Crisp in *The Naked Civil Servant* is a ground-breaking representation of a gay persons experience, and Channel 4's *Queer as Folk* set out to alter the well-worn image of the doomed homosexual in television.

Although there have been some interesting developments in gay representation in recent years, there remains a heterocentric rule in mainstream television. For example, there are main protagonists who are gay in certain sit-coms such as *Gimme Gimme Gimme* and *Will and Grace*, which is certainly a step forward, yet there are few (if any) representations of gay main characters in, for example, crime drama. Equally, there may be some openly gay chat show or game show hosts, but more 'serious' positions such as that of the newsreader, are held by (apparently) heterosexual people.

It is also worth noting that many of the representations of gay people on television take the form of gay men, with lesbianism being historically and contemporarily under-represented.

However, the plurality of television has led to some popular exceptions. As discussed earlier in this Guide, *Six Feet Under* provides a refreshingly original inclusion of gay characters and issues, including lesbianism. The popularity of *The L-Word* in the United States and in Britain may also point to the fact that the public is ready to deal with more complex and long running television depicting gay women.

Marxism

Marxism has evolved from the thesis of Marx and Engels into a means of foregrounding economic and social issues across culture and art. Marxism has had a fundamental influence on film theory and criticism, not least because the concept of ideology is central to the analysis. The core issue of the organisation of power and the class system remains the focus of Marxist approaches to film, and can be seen on a number of levels, as I shall discuss. Although not entirely relevant to the GCSE / A level Media and Film student, it should be noted that some film-makers have worked in an *explicitly* Marxist context, using the form as a means of expounding the political manifesto of socialism. The Russian Formalist movement of the 1920s, as undertaken by film-makers such as Sergei Eisenstein, took place in the context of a Socialist movement, and can be considered as a real alternative to the mainly capitalist Hollywood output. As with many other aspects of film theory, the all-important 1970s galvanised the area as a useful way of approaching cinema. Marxism and class is best approached as another way by which the ideological implications of a text and its mode of production are scrutinised, and works well as a theoretical companion to the issues of race, gender, sexuality, nationality, etc.

The following is a framework for approaching Marxism in film.

Ideology

A Marxist approach to film seeks to foreground the issues of class and hegemony and explores the ideological stance that the film apparently endorses or criticises. This can be an approach which focuses on film-makers who are working with an explicitly political agenda, such as Ken Loach or Michael Moore. Alternatively, it can be a means of approaching the subtext of the given film. For example, **Starship Troopers** (1997) can be seen as a thinly veiled attack on right wing America posing as a science fiction epic. Marxism can also be used as a means of critically viewing other texts as endorsements of capitalist ideology. For example, *Jerry Maguire* (1996) can be seen as an endorsement of capitalist ideology where the individual can thrive and benefit from competition and innovation. More complex issues are explored in such films as **The Matrix**, which whilst on the one hand – as a text – appears to be critical of the loss of individuality in the capitalist world (with human beings literally being used as a resource); on the other hand – as a commercial Hollywood product – includes product placement and begat a lucrative franchise.

Other films simply foreground the subject of class as a central theme. For example, **Rocky** (1976), **Trading Places** (1983) and **Pretty Woman** (1990) all concern on a narrative level the issue of class without working in an explicitly political context.

Industry

The film industry is a huge financial network fuelled by the goal of profit, and therefore it is natural that Marxism provides a critique of the industrialisation of the art form. On one level, all films can be seen as coming from different outposts of the wider film industry. As such, Hollywood can be seen as producing a certain number of films that come through the studio system, and this can affect film-making trends as well as what is or is not sanctioned as a viable economic option. For example, there is currently a proliferation of films adapted from comic books (for instance, **X-Men** (2000), **Spider-Man**, **Hellboy**, **Batman Begins** (2005)). This trend is essentially market led, and is profitable and ultimately desirable from a studio point of view because of the huge moneymaking franchise surrounding these productions. As depressing as it may seem, a major Hollywood film is now judged by executives partly based on its 'toyality', that is, the merchandising options that it creates. This has led some to criticise the 'McDonaldsisation' of the film industry. It can be argued, for example, that the inclusion of a lengthy pod race sequence in **Star Wars Episode I: The Phantom Menace** (1999) is little more than an advertisement for the video game tie-in which was released at the same time as the film.

It is also worth considering the alternatives to mainstream Hollywood output. Independent cinema exists in part as a means of approaching subject matter that is deemed taboo to the, at times, formulaic Hollywood film, and independent film and film-makers have been crucial in the development of an artistic vanguard. In contemporary cinema, it is also advisable to be aware of the way the current American industry works, with many seemingly 'independent' production companies actually being owned and influenced by a larger corporate parent company (as in Miramax Films, owned by Disney, or New Line, part of Time Warner).

There are also clear alternatives to the Hollywood studio system. Bollywood cinema's global presence cannot be ignored, nor can the huge Hong Kong film industry. There are also national outputs, which constitute an important part of the global network. As discussed earlier, film-makers such as Ken Loach have used film as a tool for critiquing the dominant social status quo, and have worked outside of the mainstream whilst managing to comment upon it. Others have managed this within the context of mainstream US cinema. For example, the film-maker Michael Moore has managed to critique the dominant American political institution whilst distributing the work through (allegedly with some difficulty) the dominant studio system. Other film-makers have managed to criticise the economic constraints of film-making itself. For example, Robert Altman provided a critical assessment of the dominance of economic factors in Hollywood with *The Player* (1992).

Audience

This involves taking into account a number of factors. For example, the demographic that a mainstream film is pitched at will affect the content and marketing it receives. Consider a film such as Pixar's *Finding Nemo* (2003), which is an example of marketing genius at work. Aimed primarily at young children, the film involves the generic template of a youngster and parent being separated only to be reunited after a journey (as seen in *The Land Before Time* (1988) and *Ice Age* (2002)). This film is aggressively marketed to children and as a result, only the most cold-hearted of parents would fail to take their offspring to the multiplex to see the film. The result is a marketing dream, with families rather than individuals paying out to see a single film and the lucrative DVD release grossing millions. The merchandise that can be tied-into these films is also of huge importance to studios, which can multiply the amount available from box office returns alone. Other films are also marketed to clearly identifiable audiences or demographics: the 'chick flick', the teen movie and the romantic comedy are all made with a specific audience in mind, whilst the crossover appeal of films such as *Lord of The Rings* and *Titanic* remain the holy grail of the film industry.

On a practical level, it is desirable that students can take a step back from any given text and look at the wider context of the film and the way it is operates in the industry as a part of a huge media network. The ability to conduct close textual analysis in tandem with wider contextual factors makes for a well-rounded academic approach to media texts.

Marxism and Television

As is the case with postmodernism, television throws up its own particular issues concerning class and power because of its mass appeal and circulation. No other media format is accessed on such an everyday level, and it is worth considering this when approaching Marxism and television. The same principle frameworks of analysis outlined above can be applied to television.

Regarding ideology, texts can be approached either as representations of class and power, or alternatively critically approached as hegemonic ideological tools. For example, working class life has long been represented in television in many forms, from documentary, soaps, dramas or comedy. Certain television landmarks have directly addressed issues surrounding working class people in an overtly politicised manner. Ken Loach's seminal TV films *Cathy Come Home* (1966) and *Poor Cow* (1967) acted as a shot in the arm to British broadcasting, teaching many that television was a suitable format for approaching serious issues such as class, and marked a pivotal turning point in the history of British broadcasting. Other fictions have approached the subject of class in a less overtly political, but nonetheless vital manner. For example, Roddy Doyle's *Family*, an intimate portrayal of poverty and familial relationships on a council estate in Dublin. Recent interesting examples include *Shameless*, discussed as a case study later, and *City of Men*, a spin-off series from the film **City of God** (2002).

Working class life is not the only area of representation appropriate to a Marxist approach to analysis. Some dramas concern the upper echelons of the class system and the corruption that power can bring. Dramas such as *House of Cards* and *State of Play* have dealt with corruption in the political system, and use power and wealth as a source of drama.

It is not only in drama that the representation of class can be seen. Indeed some genres of television seem well suited to representing class as a source of interest and humour. The most popular soap operas in Britain have dealt mainly with working class people: the longevity of *Coronation Street* and *EastEnders* attest to the public's interests in the activities and interests of working class characters. Interestingly, many long running American serials that have been popular in Britain have concerned wealthier people and their environments. Take, for example, the success of *Dallas* and *Dynasty*, and more recently *The OC*. Sitcoms have also embraced class as a field of interest. From *Steptoe and Son, To the Manor Born, Only Fools and Horses, Absolutely Fabulous* and *The Royle Family*, class has been the basis of the situation that characters find themselves in.

We may also wish to consider the messages that some non-fiction television programmes are sending out. Take, for example, the proliferation of programmes designed to give people a leg up in the capitalist rat race. The upsurge and popularity of property development based programmes illustrate the public thirst for competitive strategies in an economic sense. Perhaps the prime contender for the most aggressively capitalist show on Earth is the US import *The Apprentice*, which gives would-be young executives the chance to impress billionaire Donald Trump (or Alan Sugar in the British re-make) by trouncing their rivals in business.

Two vast areas that are not addressed in detail here are certainly worth considering with regards to a Marxist approach to the media. One is that of advertising, as both a purveyor of aspirational lifestyles and the scheduling around which it rotates. Another is the area of institutions and industries, where the workings behind organisations such as the BBC and Sky are a good source of study.

3.2 Case Studies

The critical approaches and theories discussed thus far are not intended to be a concrete set of theses that should be necessarily taught in a formal context. Rather, they exist as a collection of often interconnected ideas about film-making that simply seek to create an intellectual basis for approaching the moving image. It is key to note that no one approach exists alone as an empirical and definitive approach that is the 'right' way of looking at film and television. It should also be remembered that they often overlap in their ideas. For example, psychoanalysis informs feminism, which in turn informs and influences queer theory.

It may be that the terminology and specialised language surrounding these ideas are helpful in disseminating this information: however, it can also get in the way of delivering the essence of the ideas themselves. It is more advisable to see these theories as ways in which to approach a text, each foregrounding a different aspect of the text itself. As such, one can take a feminist, structuralist, Marxist, etc. approach to any given text in order to draw out and foreground a particular aspect. The following are case studies to which differing critical approaches are applied.

Erin Brockovich

Erin Brockovich – *fusing mainstream entertainment and social commentary*

Directed by Steven Soderbergh and starring Julia Roberts as the eponymous heroine, **Erin Brockovich** is based upon true events of a legal secretary's prominence in a case against corporate America. The film won many plaudits from critics and a Best Actress Academy Award for Roberts, and restored Soderbergh to the role of 'A'-list director after a period in the critical and commercial doldrums. The film centres on the character of Brockovich, a down on her luck single mother who begins the film by being involved in a car accident. After her lawyer (played by Albert Finney) fails to win her damages that she believes she deserves, she demands that his firm gives her a job. While investigating a property rights case, she uncovers evidence that a manufacturing firm has poisoned the water supply of a local community and lied to sick residents in its aftermath. Brockovich then investigates a huge cover up and is involved in the legal case that sees the poor local residents take on, and beat, the corporate machine.

The film is an interesting fusion of mainstream entertainment and social commentary, and works both in the context of a legal drama and a politicised attack on corporate greed. In this aspect it resembles Soderbergh's *Traffic* (2000), which is a similar blend of entertainment and commentary. It also began the working relationship between Roberts and the director, for who she represents something of a muse. They have since worked together on another three occasions, in *Full Frontal* (2002), *Ocean's Eleven* and *Ocean's Twelve* (2004).

Erin Brockovich can be considered in the context of the more poetic *Thelma and Louise*, in that it is a major Hollywood production from a leading director, which centres on a woman's struggle against the prevailing society of the day. But whereas *Thelma and Louise* ends on a tragic and metaphoric note, with the women driving off a cliff top into the great blue yonder (and into the collective imagination) rather than accede to the constraints of society, *Erin Brockovich* sees the heroine succeed in her goal and win one for the common people.

The following is a framework of analysis in which a range of approaches can be used in order to privilege and foreground certain aspects of the film. This is to demonstrate the ways in which multiple readings of a given text can be used for the purpose of critical reception. No single reading should be viewed in dogmatic terms as fixed and more 'correct' than another. Similarly, the terminology used should be available as a tool if required rather than the received system to be imposed. The ability to approach a text in a number of ways is the intended outcome here, in order to allow students to have a well-rounded and objective understanding of texts.

Feminism

Erin Brockovich is an affirmative story of a woman's fight to gain recognition in a male dominated corporate environment. It is important to note that the main protagonist is fighting for the rights of working class families that have little or no clout in the corporate world, which mirrors her own experiences as a single mother out of work. She achieves her goals with singular vision, intelligence and compassion, rather than by becoming as ruthless and cut-throat as her male competitors. The main character is confident and sharp, and does not rely upon her physical attributes to win support. Although she dresses in a style which some would see as 'trashy' or revealing, it is made clear that this is out of personalised style and choice rather than from a position of objectification. This is mirrored in the filming style, where she is not positioned as an object of desire but more as a leading figure and vocal presence.

The film is thoroughly centred on the lead character, and the *mise-en-scène* is focused on her in practically every frame. As such, we gain information from the worldview of the female lead, and are positioned as viewers firmly (and unusually in terms of Hollywood) from her perspective. The film also presents the dilemma of child rearing and career building in Erin's struggle to balance these two aspects of her life. In doing so it offers a genuine and alternative path, with Erin's boyfriend (played by Aaron Eckhart) taking responsibility for domestic issues and child rearing.

The film also demonstrates that a female lead can carry a box office hit, and one that deals with 'serious' social issues at that. Roberts demonstrates her ongoing screen potential, acting ability and star quality, and breaks free from the role of romantic interest that she has played in other films. It is also worth noting that although the film is directed by a man, it is written by a woman as well as being based upon the experiences of a real person. Overall, the film presents a positive role model for women which is made all the more significant by its semi-autobiographical content.

Marxism

The film can be seen as essentially a battle between the oppressed working class and the corporate machine, which places little or no value on their existence. It is important to note that the working class heroine helps others in a similar position as herself, and it is through unity and mutual understanding that they succeed against the corporation. As well as being an attack on corporate greed and mismanagement, the film also champions the rights of those that would be silenced by the imbalanced American legal system.

The film is a part of a trend in turn of the millennium American cinema, which used the genre of the semi-autobiographical thriller as a means of conveying a critical comment on corporate America. Other films in this small but significant group include **The Insider** (1999), which dealt with the tobacco industry, and **A Civil Action** (1999), which dealt with the corporate dumping of toxic waste. These films are reminders that although working within a studio system that essentially sells entertainment for the purpose of economic revenue, film has revolutionary potential and the ability to inform vast audiences of the injustices of corporate America. This trend follows on from such legal dramas as **Philadelphia**, which have a long tradition of representing the plight of the individual facing the might of the corporate machine. This notion of the individual against the system can be traced back to Frank Capra's loose trilogy (**Mr Deeds Goes to Town** (1936), **Meet John Doe** (1941), **Mr Smith Goes to Washington** (1939)), which exhibits a strong socio-political conscience.

Psychoanalysis

The film can be seen as a character study that represents the singular view of the main protagonist. As such, the characteristics of determination, intelligence and compassion are drawn out through the script and performance. The film also explores the emotion of grief, as seen in the loss that is felt by those families whose relatives have died as a result of the poisoning of the water supply. On the other hand, it also represents the coldness and callousness of those involved in the corporation, and raises the moral issue of responsibility for corporate decisions, as well as the monetary value of human life. **Erin Brockovich** is a moral tale of the rights of the individual faced with odds against them, and the fight for justice in modern America.

The viewer is positioned in such a way as to feel an almost instant empathy towards the main protagonist. This is achieved in a number of ways. Firstly, some viewers would approach this film with existing knowledge of the real Erin Brockovich, whose story has become a popular truism of the fight of the determined individual against the odds. Secondly, as the title suggests, the film is centred on the main character. As we have a natural propensity to seek to affiliate ourselves to the central character in film, we instantly seek to side with Erin. This is made all the easier by the clear moral austerity of her struggle, and the negative depiction of the corporation as an unfeeling and callous group. Thirdly, the fact that the star of the film is Julia Roberts should not be ignored. Most viewers would have an existing familiarity with the actress, and will recognise her performance on some level as exactly that. It should be noted that throughout her career, Roberts has rarely played a villain or character with negative connotations associated with them, and so a viewer may have a natural tendency to side with her out of habit.

The three approaches to **Erin Brockovich** outlined above are appropriate to the text, and are of some use in finding ways of drawing certain aspects of the film to the forefront. Others are applicable (such as auteur theory in the case of Soderbergh) depending on the given text.

Whereas a structuralist approach to textual analysis (as outlined in Chapter 1) is useful in decoding and identifying the codes and conventions of the moving image, this critical approach is useful in dealing with the issues and debates surrounding cinematic reading. The goal should be a marriage of close stylistic interpretation of the formal aspects of film-making and the ability to deal with the prevalent and underlying ideas with which a text presents us.

Shameless

First aired in January 2004, *Shameless* is a Channel 4 production, which takes the form of seven, one hour dramas. *Shameless* is the first show written for the channel by Paul Abbott, the acclaimed writer of the BBC's *Clocking Off* and *Linda Green*. The programme is set in contemporary Manchester, and focuses on one family (the Gallaghers) who live on an inner-city council estate.

Shameless is a blend of drama and comedy, with the harsher realities of working class life being offset by the humorous situations the characters find themselves in. In particular, the antics of the wayward father, Frank, provide a vast source of entertainment and amusement. *Shameless* has proved a success for Channel 4, and headed up their festive 2004 line up with a Christmas special. The second series (2005) continues this success, and the programme looks set to leave a mark on the TV landscape.

Marxism

Shameless is essentially an examination of characters existing on the margins of mainstream society. Fiona is struggling to bring up her family in the face of adversity because of the economic constraints imposed by the absence of a familial structure in which they might be financially provided for. That is, struggling and succeeding in the face of such adversity. Although life is difficult, the Gallaghers remain extremely close and pull together, their strength coming from shared unity. Financial concerns exist on a level of everyday detail, with, for example, the children riffling through the pockets of their drunken father in order to obtain money for school. Fiscal concerns also exist on a broader narrative level, with the climax of the first series being the growing financial independence of the family, in which Steve buys a council house as a marital gift for Fiona.

The socio-economic contexts in which the characters live affect almost every storyline, indeed the entire premise of the series being their refusal to bow in the face of their situation (a 'shameless' celebration of life and family). For example, after meeting Fiona in a nightclub, Steve becomes fascinated with the Gallagher family as well as falling in love her. One of the ways in which he attempts to woo Fiona is by replacing the household washing machine, which is on its last legs. In another example, Frank fakes his own death in order to avoid paying his debts.

Shameless can also be considered as a part of an ongoing representation by British television of working class life and working class people in non-reductive terms. In this sense, the comedic framework in which it operates should not detract from its credentials as a bona-fide step forward in terms of television. It can be considered, therefore, alongside the likes of Alan Bleasdale's *Boys from the Black Stuff* and Roddy Doyle's *Family*, both as an artistic presentation of working class family life and as a testament to television's ability to tackle serious issues using a populist model.

Queer theory

One of the interesting things worth considering with regards to *Shameless* is the way in which it includes gay identity into its milieu without making an overtly ideological statement about the fact. Whereas previous landmarks in gay representation such as *Queer as Folk* brought the issue to the forefront and gained notoriety not least because of their historical significance, *Shameless* includes the issue in real terms without being dominated by it.

Specifically, three characters highlight the issue of gay identity. Ian Gallagher is a young man coming to terms with his own emergent homosexuality in a family where gay identity is not high on the agenda. Whilst working at the local grocery shop, Ian has been having an affair with Kash, an older married Muslim man closeted in a loveless marriage. Frank's estranged wife Monica returns to the family in the later episodes of the first series, causing much commotion, not least because of the fact that she returns with her lesbian lover, Norma.

As such, three interesting areas of lesbian and gay identity are encountered in *Shameless*. These are:

- Ian's sexual orientation explored in the context of working class family life and in particular with regards to the relationship between him and his straight brother, Lip. After finding pornography in the room he shares with Ian, Lip has to come to terms with his brother's homosexuality. This, like all other issues in the series, is dealt with candidly, in terms of both language and humour, as the brothers find their own way to discuss and explore their own emergent sexuality.

- The issue of closeted sexuality encountered in Kash, whose marriage sees him live a dual identity both as a family man with a business to run and an active homosexual with a secret lover. This also illuminates the issue of homosexuality in other cultures or in a racially/culutrally diverse society, where Kash's desire for a family, and not least his heterosexuality, is taken as a given.

- The issue of an older woman's sexual re-orientation into a lesbian love affair, raised when Monica returns to the family. The return to the familial home necessitates her children not only to deal with the presence of a mother that they had learnt to live without, but also the fact that she is involved in a same-sex relationship. Again, this is dealt in a candid tone, in which a previously taboo subject is faced head on as a facet of modern life.

Auteur theory

The series can also be considered as a part of the trajectory of Paul Abbot's career, one of the few contemporary contenders for the position of genuine television auteur. From *Coronation Street* to *Clocking Off* to *Linda Green,* Abbot has provided an interested and challenging take on working class life (and specifically the Northern working classes), providing his audience with three dimensional characters who remain entertaining and perhaps most importantly believable, without being presented in an overtly didactic politicised form.

Selected Bibliography

Allen, R. and Hill, A. (eds) *The Television Studies Reader,* London: Routledge, 2003.

Andrew, J. D. *The Major Film Theories: An Introduction,* Oxford: Oxford University Press, 1976.

Barthes, R. *Mythologies,* London: Seuil Publishers, 1970.

Bordwell, D. and Thomson. K. *Film Art and Film History: An Introduction,* New York: Macmillan Higher Education, 2003.

Bordwell, D. *Narration in the Fiction Film,* London: Routledge, 1987.

Branston, G. Stafford, R. *The Media Students Book,* London: Routledge, 1996.

Brunsdon, C. et al *Feminist Television Criticism: A Reader,* Oxford: Oxford University Press, 1997.

Brunsdon, C. (ed.) *Films for Women,* London: BFI, 1986.

Brunsdon, C. *The Feminist, the Housewife and the Soap Opera,* Oxford: Oxford University Press, 2000.

Bryant, J. Zillman, D. *Media Effects: Advances in Theory and Research,* London: Lawrence Erlbaum Associates, 1994.

Butler, J. *Gender Trouble: Feminism and the Subversion of Identity,* New York: Routledge, 1990.

Carstarphen, M. and Zavoina, S. *Sexual Rhetoric: Media Perspectives on Sexuality, Gender, and Identity,* Greenwood Press, 1999.

Clarke, D. (ed.) *The Cinematic City,* London: Routledge, 1997.

Coover, G. 'Television and Social Identity: Race Representation as "White" Accommodation', *Journal of Broadcasting & Electronic Media, Vol. 45,* 2001.

Creeber, G. (ed.) *The Television Genre Handbook*, London: BFI, 2001.

Eldridge, J. Kitzinger, J. Williams, K. *The Mass Media and Power in Modern Britain*, Oxford: Oxford University Press, 1997.

Gehring, W. *The Handbook of American Film Genres*, Greenwood Press, 1988.

Gever, M., Greyson, J. and Parma, P. (eds) *Queer Looks: Perspectives in Lesbian and Gay Film and Video*, New York: Routledge, 1993.

Hayward, S. *Cinema Studies: The Key Concepts*, London: Routledge, 2000.

Herman, W. *Film and the Critical Eye*, London: Macmillan, 1975.

Hill, J and Church Gibson, P. (eds) *The Oxford Companion to Film Studies*, Oxford: Oxford University Press, 1998.

Hood, S. *On Television*, London: Pluto Press, 1980.

Humm. M. *Feminism and Film*, Edinburgh: Edinburgh University Press, 1997.

Izod, J. *Reading the Screen*, Harlow: Longman, 1989.

Jancovich, M and Hollows, J. (eds) *The Film Studies Reader*, London: Hodder Arnold, 2000.

Kracauer, S. *Theory of Film: The Redemption of Physical Reality*, Oxford: Oxford University Press, 1974.

Lowe. B. *Media Mythologies*, University of New South Wales Press, 1995.

Mast, G., Cohen, M. and Braudy, L. (eds) *Film Theory and Criticism*, Oxford: Oxford University Press, 1992.

McDonald, M. *Representing Women*, London: Arnold, 1995.

McQuillan, M. *The Narrative Reader*, London: Routledge, 2000.

McRobbie, A. *Postmodernism and Popular Culture*, London: Routledge, 1994.

Miller, T. (ed.) *Television Studies*, London: BFI Publishing, 2003.

Morley, D. *Television Audiences and Cultural Studies*, London: Routledge, 1992.

Mulvey, L. 'Visual Pleasure and Narrative Cinema', *Screen* 16 (3), autumn 1975 and Braudy L. & Cohen, M. (eds) *Film Theory and Criticism* (5th ed.), Oxford: OUP, 1999

Neale, S. *Cinema and Technology: Image, Sound, Colour,* London: Macmillan, 1985.

Nelmes, J. (ed.) *An Introduction to Film Studies,* London: Routledge, 1996.

O'Sullivan, T., and Jewkes, Y. *The Media Studies Reader,* London: Arnold, 1997.

Real, M. R. *Exploring Media Culture: A Guide,* London: Sage, 1996.

Sarup, M. *An Introductory Guide to Post-Structuralism and Postmodernism,* New York: Harvester Wheatsheaf, 1988.

Stead, P. *Film and the Working Class,* London: Routledge, 1989.

Sontag, S. *Against Interpretation,* London: Picador, 2001.

Shaheen, J. *Reel Bad Arabs: How Hollywood Vilifies a People,* Arris Books, 2003.

Stevenson, G. *Understanding Media Cultures: Social Theory and Mass Communication,* London: Sage, 1995.

Thornham, S. (ed.) *Feminist Film Theory: A Reader,* Edinburgh: Edinburgh University Press, 1999.

Tasker, Y. *Spectacular Bodies: Gender, Genre and Action Cinema,* London: Routledge, 1993.

Turner, G. *Film as Social Practice,* London: Routledge, 1993.

Williams, R. *Television, Technology and Cultural Form, Second Edition,* London: Routledge, 1990.

Willis, S. *High Contrast: Race and Gender in Contemporary Hollywood Film,* Duke University Press, 1997.

http://www.thirdway.org/files/articles/antiarab.html

Links

Based upon the Dewey System, here are some suggestions for where relevant sections can be located in your library:

- Media 302.23
- Advertising 302.23
- TV, Radio and Film and 791.43 and 791.45
- Television 302.2345 and 791.45
- Culture 306
- Film 791

Journals and Newspapers

- Creative Review
- Empire Magazine
- In the Picture
- Media Magazine
- Sight and Sound
- Televisual
- The Guardian (Monday's Media Supplement)
- The Observer
- The Sunday Times (first issue of the month carries a free CD with media resources)

Reference

- 'Issues' series
- Whitakers Almanac
- The Media Guide
- Film Guides

Web

- www.theory.org
- www.guardian.co.uk
- www.empireonline.co.uk
- www.imdb.com

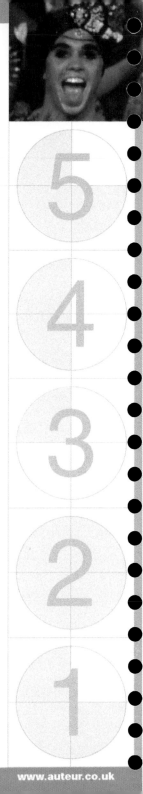

Film and Television Textual Analysis
A Teacher's Guide
Keith McDonald

Film and Television Textual Analysis: A Teacher's Guide provides the Film, Media Studies and English teacher with a comprehensive introduction to the subject and a range of approaches to teaching the analysis of the moving image. The **Guide** introduces the key concepts and analytical tools required, and explores ways in which they can be applied to the study of the media and film in the classroom. It is structured in three parts:

- an introduction to the core concepts, practices and terminologies;
- an exploration of the ideas, issues and debates that stem from textual analysis, including representation, genre and ideology;
- an introduction to the key theories and critical approaches, including feminist theory, psychoanalysis, Marxism, structuralism and auteur theory.

Throughout, a range of popular and accessible case studies are used, including *The Matrix Reloaded*, *Six Feet Under*, *Moulin Rouge*, *Sweet Sixteen* and *Shameless*. All of the concepts and approaches in the book are discussed in the context of clear examples to both older and contemporary texts.

This **Teacher's Guide** is the ideal primer for those approaching the subject for the first time and an up-to-date handbook for the more experienced teacher.

Keith McDonald teaches English Literature and English Language at York College and is completing a PhD in AIDS and Representation.

Also available

Film and Television Textual Analysis
Classroom Resources
Keith McDonald

The highly practical **Classroom Resources** are designed for use in tandem with the **Teacher's Guide**. Included are a comprehensive set of handouts and task sheets offering a range of activities and information designed to help students understand and explore textual analysis.

Cover photograph: *Moulin Rouge* (2001), courtesy of Moviestore Collection.

ISBN 1-903663-53-9

9 781903 663530

Auteur Publishing   www.auteur.co.uk